ASSEMBLY LINE

TEACHING THE BIBLE IN ASSEMBLIES

Written by Andrew Smith

With contributions from David Bell, Steve Tilley, Malcolm Raby, Simon Heathfield and Nigel Harris.

Pathfinders

Contents

Assembles are boring!

This comment was repeated again and again in the survey I did in preparation for this book. Assemblies were generally considered to be boring and irrelevant. **Assembly Line** has been written in part to try to counter that attitude. It has been written with a conviction that God's message in the Bible is relevant for all people, and can be taught sensitively, acceptably and interestingly in assemblies. **Assembly Line** has also been put together to help you teach about some of the great truths in the Bible by looking at Biblical characters. By doing this you will also be retelling some of the great stories of the Bible: stories that many young people will never have heard.

As well as the assembly outlines, there are the **Nuts & Bolts** pages. These cover different issues to help you make your assemblies even better. Some of the issues you will probably already have thought about and found your own solutions to, but there may be new ideas for even the most seasoned assembly leader. The **Nuts & Bolts** pages also help to explain how some of the ideas in the assemblies can be made to work effectively.

Assemblies come in all shapes and sizes, no two are ever the same. To try to provide a resource that is as useful as possible, I have written the assemblies with the aim of making them adaptable. Some assemblies last half an hour, others are only ten minutes long, so any resource which is to meet both of these needs has to be flexible. As you plan your assemblies think about the time, skills and facilities you have at your disposal, so that you can adapt the assemblies as you need to. Leave out those parts which you do not have time for, or you are unable to use. You can then save them to use on another occasion.

This might sound like hard work for something that lasts less than half an hour at the start of the day. But the way Christianity is taught and presented in those few minutes can make a crucial difference to the pupils. If their only experience of Christianity is ill-prepared boring assemblies, they will soon conclude that it is Christianity which is at fault. But if what they experience is interesting and relevant, who can tell what it might lead to? There needs to be a move away from thinking, 'Oh it's only an assembly, I'll prepare it in the morning before I go,' to a more thought-out, constructive approach. This might sound idealistic in a world where everyone is already too busy, but if assemblies are to be appealing to the pupils they will need preparing. You may be one of those fortunate people who can turn up at five minutes' notice and deliver a stunning, fun, relevant assembly, (in which case, you probably haven't even bought this book), but for the rest of us a really good assembly needs preparation. After all, 'Assemblies could be worthwhile if more time was spent preparing them.'

What do pupils want from assemblies?

In preparation for this resource, I undertook a survey of over 100 pupils. They came from a variety of schools in a range of social situations. Sadly, most of them said that on the whole they didn't enjoy assemblies. The overwhelming reason for this was that the pupils considered them to be boring. Below is a summary of the results I had. If we are going to overcome pupils' perception of assemblies as boring we need to listen to what they want and use those ideas where appropriate. The two most popular ideas for what pupils would like to happen were drama, both watching and taking part in it, and having pupils involved in the assemblies.

What makes pupils laugh in assemblies

Funny personal stories
Drama
Jokes
Silly drawings
Mistakes
Silly costumes
Conjuring
Certain people are seen as people who make you laugh or think

What makes pupils think in assemblies

Praying
Talking about God and Jesus
Talks about what is happening in the world
Stories about animals
Assemblies about poor people or other countries
A radio broadcast
Having animals in the assembly
Issues like cancer
Stories with meanings

What pupils do not like in assemblies

Boring assemblies
Long boring speeches
Stuff about sport
No pupil involvement
Notices
Repetition
Just people talking
Talks about school rules
Not meaning anything
Stories
No effort put into them
Being laughed at
Praying
Bible Stories

What pupils like in assemblies

Singing
Certain people
Stories
Morals at the end of stories
Acting
Visits from clergy
Harvest appeal
Stories of people's youth
Animals in the assemblies
Orchestra
Pupils imitating the staff
Getting certificates
Watching drama

What else pupils would like to see happen in assemblies

Plays
Pupils getting involved
More fast songs
Stories
Debates
Discussion
People telling stories rather than reading them
More awards
Watching videos
Quizzes
Listening to music
Singing
Making them understandable
Funny things
Dance
Visitors

How can I use an OHP in assemblies?

Many schools have overhead projectors and these can be used to enhance what you are doing in an assembly. Below are some tips on how to make the most of the OHP. If you are going to be preparing slides to use, (this is what the acetates are called when they have been drawn or written on), it is nearly always worth doing them with a permanent pen. This means that they will not get washed away and you can keep them to use another time. Pictures can be very versatile and adapted to a whole variety of different uses.

Preparation Tips

◆ The glass platform of your projector will be slightly smaller than your acetate sheet, so leave a margin round the edge.

◆ If you are filling in an outline of a picture you have traced or drawn, you will find that the second colour will smudge the marks made by the first pen. The secret is to turn the slide over and colour in on the other side. You can also highlight words or phrases in this way.

◆ If you want to wipe away part of a slide, prepare the slide with permanent pens, and then add the parts to be removed with a water-based pen so that they can be removed with a damp cloth.

◆ Most plain paper photocopiers will produce OHP slides on specially designed A4 acetate sheets. Although these are more expensive than ordinary acetates they have many advantages. The quality of your slides improves, and they take a lot less time to prepare than hand drawing or tracing a picture.

Presentation Tips

◆ You can have several sheets of acetate on one slide, so that information can be built up bit by bit.

◆ Acetate sheets can be attached to cardboard frames. This makes them easier to file and more convenient to use.

◆ Parts of a framed slide can be hidden under taped paper 'flaps', and uncovered when required. This is a more reliable method of revealing parts of a slide than merely sliding a loose piece of paper across it.

◆ If you need several flaps on one slide stick the last one in position first, and overlay this with the preceding one, and so on. They will then lift off easily, in the right order, without revealing chinks of light.

◆ You can move characters around on the glass platform to make it look as if they are moving across the screen. It's corny but fun and always gets a groan. To do this, make the person no larger than a quarter of the size of the glass platform and use a piece of acetate longer than the person. You can then move it across the glass platform without your hand being seen. When the person goes a different way, just turn the picture over and it has changed direction. Again, it's corny, but people like it.

◆ You can make pictures more interesting by using 'masks'. These are paper silhouettes taped to a cardboard frame. You can then add acetate pictures to the slide. For example, by having 'masks' of trees, you can move an acetate character across the frame making it look as if it is hiding behind trees.

◆ You can do other visual jokes with an OHP: simple things like turning it off if there's a night scene in a story; having a small 'mask' of a boat which you can move around to make it look as if it's on a rough sea; or having a small picture of the sun which you move up and down the glass platform depending on the time of day of your story.

◆ You can get really adventurous and have two OHPs. You can then have a character on each OHP as if they are talking to each other, or use copies of pictures to make it look as if someone has moved from one OHP to the other. You do this by sliding the picture off one side of one OHP as a copy is slid onto the other. You need to practise this to make sure they go on and off the correct sides.

Can I plan a series of assemblies?

Assemblies are short and very occasionally sweet. All the attention-getting and zany ideas from **Assembly Line** need to be crammed into very little time. One way to overcome the difficulty is to lead a series of linked assemblies for the same pupils. The series might be three assemblies in one week, or an assembly once a month, but the aim is to make even more of an impact by building up and reinforcing both the message and the relationships with the young people and the school.

There are many advantages of doing a series.

◆ It means that you can deal with things in more depth – building from one assembly to the next.

◆ You can reinforce one message by repetition and tackle the same thing from different angles.

◆ You will be able to make the assemblies more interactive because you know what will work.

◆ Spending time with one group will give you a chance to get to know the pupils.

◆ Running a series may well also build up expectations in the pupils for your next assembly.

◆ One big advantage is that the school knows what to expect: that you are responsible and competent.

But there are some difficulties. Do not assume everything you did last time will be clearly remembered, and do not forget that some pupils will have been away. Avoid too much predictability, and if you feel it has gone badly once, then you will feel the need to catch up lost ground next time.

You need to plan how the methods of presentation used in a series of assemblies will relate to each other, to help you link the assemblies together. One extreme is to make the techniques used as different as possible. The other is to work to a fixed format which is exactly the same on each occasion. Usually, you will want to go for a mixture of the two. Some ideas for creating links are:

◆ Produce a soap opera with an episode in each assembly. You could do a spoof on a current favourite, or make up your own.

◆ Let the pupils get to know you by taking along an item of yours which you can use to relate the main point of the assembly to your own experience.

◆ Do interviews with different people but ask them the same questions. This helps to make sure that you link what you are doing to real Christian experience.

◆ Have a question time – invite the pupils to give you written questions the week before and then select some to answer. If some of the stupid questions you get are witty it would be good to answer some of those, in an appropriate way!

◆ Find an opportunity to get some quick vox-pop reactions on video from the pupils. Edit this into something snappy to show next time. You will need TV equipment sufficient for the number of people in the assembly. You need to think of a good question and ask it of everyone.

If you don't want to spend time recapping what happened in a previous assembly, have something visual you used last time to do the job for you. It could be a picture, a prop, or anything else you can have there without needing to draw attention to it.

Or... almost anything else from your presentation can be used in the same way to make a link... music, gags, games, jokes, jingles etc.

Do the basic planning for the whole series at once, so that you know how if fits together. But don't do all the detailed planning until you see how it is going. Evaluation is particularly important if you are planning a series, so that you can make the most of the next assemblies. See **Nuts & Bolts** page 61 for ideas on how to do this.

For ideas on some assembly series turn to **Nuts & Bolts** page 57

REMEMBER

- **In a series you can deal with things in more depth.**
- **You will have the opportunity to get to know the pupils.**
- **You should avoid too much predictability.**
- **You must plan how the methods of presentation help to link assemblies together.**
- **Some pupils will have been away last time.**

What is the difference between religion in schools and in church?

People are asked to take assemblies for different reasons. It may be that you have been invited as a minister. After all, you are used to preaching, so an assembly should not really pose any great problems. But assemblies are not church services and need to be handled differently. So what are the differences, and how can we tackle them?

The main difference is that pupils in school have not chosen to be in an assembly. Yes, there is the opt-out clause for parents to exclude children from Christian teaching and worship, but in reality very few parents take such a stand. Children of Christian parents might reasonably argue that they have been brought to church rather than having chosen to come. But, generally speaking, people attend church out of choice – and pupils attend assembly because they have to be there. The survey done in preparation for this book showed that school assemblies are not the most popular activities. Any teacher can tell you how many pupils manage to 'get lost' between the classroom and the hall.

School assemblies are often uncomfortable places – physically uncomfortable – for pupils. I appreciate that church pews are hardly the ultimate design in comfort, but they are far better than having to sit on a cold and often dirty floor for 20 minutes or so.

School assemblies are often conducted in a 'hostile' environment. Members of staff may stand around the hall with stern expressions on their faces, almost daring pupils to misbehave; there may have been a host of notices from the headteacher criticising behaviour in the corridors, complaining about litter in classrooms, warning about smoking on the school bus... at the end of which you are announced as the visiting speaker. Not surprisingly, you will not necessarily get the impression that everyone is looking forward to what you have to say – and even less so if they are sitting on the floor.

School assemblies will often include pupils of various faiths — and many with no faith at all. You will not be speaking to people with a good grounding in the Christian faith. Sometimes parents will exclude their children from the 'religious' part of the assembly. It can be quite disconcerting to see a group of students walk out the moment you are announced!

It may be reasonable to assume that in church you are speaking to Christians or at least to those who have some biblical knowledge, but such assumptions must not be made in an assembly. Even though Religious Education is a compulsory subject, you may well discover that specifically Christian teaching is hard to find on the syllabus. Moral education, personal and social education, world religions – almost anything but Christianity is taught. If advice is to be given then assume that the pupils to whom you are speaking know nothing about the Christian faith. So when talking... keep it simple.

So, you have been invited to speak to a group of potentially hostile pupils who may be physically uncomfortable, who have turned up because they are obliged to be there and who have many things on their mind – probably not the desire to take part in an act of Christian worship.

I hope you have not been put off. It is important that you are fully aware of the situation you may well be going into. Some of the problems listed above may not apply in the school to which you have been invited. If this is so, then praise God and offer a prayer for those less fortunate than yourself.

Speaking in a school assembly is a different experience from speaking in a church, but see this as a challenge to be faced and overcome, rather than an impossible obstacle. The similarity is that the people before you are in need of the good news of Jesus.

REMEMBER

- **Pupils have not chosen to be in an assembly.**
- **School assemblies are often uncomfortable places.**
- **Pupils may know nothing about the Christian faith.**
- **The school may have pupils of various faiths – and many with no faith at all.**

How can I use drama in assemblies?

When asked, many of the young people said they wanted more drama in assemblies. They enjoy watching other people on stage, particularly if it is funny. But surely it's impractical to use drama, isn't it? After all, it takes time, effort and talent to put on a play in an assembly. Well, to a certain extent it does, but there are many ways we can include drama in our assemblies which are relatively simple. There are several sketches in this book which have been written especially for assemblies. When you are doing one of the assemblies with a sketch, don't ignore it – read this page, then give it a go!

When performing a sketch in an assembly you need to bear in mind a few things. Firstly, the idea of drama is that it is dramatic, and should involve movement and action as well as things for people to say. Many sketches I have seen have been worked on with a great deal of commitment and enthusiasm by the people involved, but have been let down by having little action, so that they quickly became static and even the funniest line seemed dull. Think how you can include some movement, even if it is just getting up from a chair, or crossing over to talk to someone. Do bear in mind that young people like seeing people run around, fight and fall over. Also, if your sketch has action it will help carry it so that the lines are not all important. This helps take the pressure off those who have lines to learn. Encourage all the people in the sketch to be visual – simple props like hats or newspapers help to give character to the parts being played. Funny wigs and baggy trousers are a winner if it is laughter you are after.

Speaking in a sketch can be hard work, as lines have to be learnt and then delivered so everyone can hear, but there is no substitute for learning and practising lines. Some people find learning lines quite hard. Try reading them just before you fall asleep – it's amazing what you can remember the next day. Practice in the hall where the assembly will be, and have someone sit at the back and shout 'PARDON' whenever they can't hear. Do not forget to think about pauses and intonation. Just because they are not there in the text does not mean you cannot add them if you want to.

If you are on your own, there may be people who can help you. Do you know any pupils in the school who you can involve? Does the school have a drama group which would put the sketch on for you? Do you know any older teenagers or students who could come in and perform the sketch first thing in the morning? There may be people in your church who are free during the day who would like to get involved in something like this. Ask around, as you never know who is waiting for their opportunity for stardom! If you are going to involve others, give them plenty of warning and opportunity to rehearse the sketch. They could also be a valuable group for you to pray with about the assembly and give you feedback at the end.

Always bear in mind that young people like short, sharp things happening. Keep the sketches short so that they are left wanting more. About 3-4 minutes is a good length to aim at.

Finally, remember that young people like watching drama and it is them we are doing assemblies for. A few minutes of drama might seem to involve a lot of work, but they can be a really valuable few minutes, and the more effort put into the sketches, the better they become and the more the young people will enjoy them. As with everything else, we should be striving for great sketches, not just satisfied with mediocre ones.

REMEMBER

- **Have some action in the sketch.**
- **Be visual.**
- **Make sure people can hear what's being said.**
- **Learn the lines well.**
- **Do not go on too long.**

An insider's view of assemblies

The following article was written by Nigel Harris. He was deputy head at **Kingshurst Secondary School**, Chelmsley Wood, Solihull until 1987 and then acting head until its closure in 1988.

Most senior staff tend to view the school assembly as a necessary burden to be borne under sufferance on certain, if not all, weekdays. At its most basic, an assembly serves as a regular communication focus where the 'clients' are reminded of their corporate responsibilities to the 'firm', although such managerial exhortations tend to be rather sterile and, sometimes, even counter-productive.

The majority of senior staff certainly seek to include some uplifting theme in their assemblies in order to give a more altruistic note to the occasion. No doubt, some have an uncanny knack for finding just the right subject at short notice. In my own case, this was not true and, although I was only required to officiate once a fortnight, sometimes it was most difficult to find a topic which would be generally uplifting and still provide a moderate degree of interest. I would throw a wide net, seeking to trawl in ideas from any source.

Our assemblies were essentially secular and humanist in character, but, interestingly, though I say so with some sense of guilt, I was sometimes ready to fall back in desperation on the Bible, especially if I could recall an appropriate story, for instance, David and Goliath or the conversion of Paul. In such cases, I felt it was important to present biblical themes in a positive and contemporary setting. However, more often, I sought inspiration from a much wider field, using media material and carefully edited memoirs from personal life. Regardless of the subject, the strategy was always to move in fast with a hopefully interesting subject to try to jerk the clients out of their usual glazed apathy, push home the moral before the visors slammed shut again, and then round off with a number of key notices concerning school procedure and practice.

I hasten to add that my assemblies had not always been modelled in this fashion. Long ago, as a new deputy, I had favoured the more non-denominational Christian outline type of assembly. I have always had an enduring love for many of the old hymn tunes and, rather naively, imagined that I could pass some of the interest on to the pupils. However, after some months of wrestling with the logistics of hymn book supply and the pathetic response of the majority of senior school pupils, I decided that this was a rocky path that I would be doomed to tread alone. In fact, I felt that the Christian form of service, even in this basic format, was too important to be treated with so little regard. I should also add that, at that time, the school population was composed almost entirely of white working-class children and the multi-cultural factor had not yet assumed any great significance. In later times, this consideration did have much more influence on the character of our assemblies.

Visiting speakers, in general, were regarded by senior staff as 'manna from Heaven' for purely practical reasons. However, over the years, as an 'old pro', one did mentally tend to grade these incomers on a sliding scale according to their performance, for instance:

6/10 – representatives of police/ambulance/fire services, who usually aroused a certain degree of interest if only through providing some spectacular tales of death and destruction;

5/10 – visitors from charities and other good causes were regarded with a certain glum tolerance, although there was always the possibility that one or two exceptional younger children would be fired to undertake some sponsored action to help out;

4/10 – a local minister, very predictably, would be seen as trying to 'flog a dead horse' in most cases, but there were happy exceptions to this;

3/10 – local politicians and industrialists seldom attracted more than a flicker of irritation, unless they were offering any free samples.

A final word to all prospective visitors. In the eyes of one head teacher, a measure of real success for any visitor was the chance to be asked back for another occasion.

How can I read the Bible in assemblies?

In the survey put together for this resource, a few pupils commented on the way the Bible was read in assemblies. The comments were fairly negative and in general described the Bible reading as boring. Not many 11-14 year olds will be used to being read to, as the last time this happened was probably when they were much younger. However in **1 Timothy 4:13** Paul instructs Timothy to 'give your time and effort to the public reading of the scriptures'.

The way we read the Bible publicly will say a lot about our attitude to it, and can influence the hearers' response to the passage. If, when we read the Bible it is boring and uninteresting, the listeners will soon decide that it is the Bible itself that is at fault.

How can we make Bible readings interesting? Firstly there is nothing like practice. Practise reading the passage you are going to use, and sort out any difficult phrases or words. If you have to turn the page, know what comes next so you won't be caught out. Practise in the place you will be doing the assembly, to make sure that people can hear you and that you are speaking slowly and clearly enough.

Look at the type of writing you have got and be true to what's there. If there are emotions in the passage, express them. Don't be afraid of pauses and raising and lowering your voice to emphasise certain phrases. As we do all this we will be giving a commentary on the passage as we read, so we need to make sure we understand it.

Involve the pupils as much as possible when you are reading. Good eye contact makes a huge difference. It shows that you are interested in the listeners, and draws them in to what you are reading. If you want to involve pupils in the reading make sure they have time to practise. A popular way for readings is to split them into parts. This can be very effective but does not take away the need to practise. In fact, it increases it. A helpful resource for dramatic readings is the Dramatised Bible that splits much of the Bible up into different parts for you. See **Nuts & Bolts** page 63 for details.

Most communication today happens on several different levels, and involves sight, sounds and often action as well. It is possible to exploit this when we are reading the Bible. Having things for people to look at keeps the interest high. It can be something as simple as having the passage displayed on an OHP with significant parts highlighted. If places are mentioned have a map of the area either drawn large, or put up on the OHP. There may be pictures you can use which illustrate parts of the reading. You could try using a video while you reading – don't worry, young people are quite capable of watching a video (with the sound turned down) and listening to you at the same time. For example you could show a wildlife video whilst reading a Psalm about God's creation.

Nearly everything that young people watch or do is accompanied by background music: Again, we can use this to our benefit when reading the Bible. Just having background music playing while you read will not only make the pupils feel more comfortable, but can help give atmosphere and feeling to a passage. Try listening out for a variety of music to use: Some very current music, which the pupils may well own, can be as effective as classical or other music which we may have immediate access to.

The main thing to remember is that reading the Bible in public can be very powerful if done well, but if done poorly it can influence the hearers' view of scripture. To do it well can take time, but it is worth it, and your skill and ability will improve with time and practice.

REMEMBER

- **Make sure you understand the passage.**
- **Sort out any difficult phrases or words.**
- **Make sure you can be heard.**
- **Practise with anyone else involved.**
- **Arrange any audio or visual ideas.**

What language can I use in assemblies?

The assembly situation is different from almost any other context in which people are asked to speak (for a fuller explanation of this see **Nuts and Bolts** page 7). One of the big differences is the kind of language which can be used to express ideas. In an assembly you are presenting Christianity to a group of people, some of whom will disagree with, or even be offended by, some of the things Christians believe. Much of what you say will be different from what they have been taught as true, either at home or by other people. However, what you have to say as a Christian is as relevant and important to the pupils as it is to anybody. The important thing is that it is presented in a correct and acceptable way.

One of the big areas that you need to watch is what you describe as truth. As a Christian there will be certain things which you will believe to be true, and some of these issues are covered in this resource. For example, God loves all people, as explained in the assembly on Paul on page 19. But some of the pupils may not believe this and to stand up and declare it as true can be considered to be insensitive or even insulting. However, this does not stop us telling the pupils what we believe to be true. Therefore, the way to teach these truths in an assembly situation is to say, 'The Bible teaches that....', or 'As a Christian, I believe that...'. By using these phrases you will be stating what you believe to be true, rather than boldly stating these things to be true. In this way you can quite legitimately present Christian truths in an acceptable way.

You will also need to be careful about jargon. Do you use words which the pupils will not understand, or take to mean something else? Will all the pupils know what you mean when you use the word 'sin'? They will almost certainly have heard the word, but their understanding of it will probably be different from yours. To help the pupils learn the Bible's understanding, you need to explain what the word means. There is a thought that Christians should avoid jargon altogether, but surely it is better for the pupils to know what these words mean, so that next time they come across them, they will have a correct understanding.

It is also possible to use jargon phrases which sound sensible when you understand them, but can cause confusion when people hear them for the first time. For example the phrase 'God gave us his only Son.' When I used this phrase once, the reply I got was 'Why? Didn't God want him?' We give something away when we no longer want it. To the young person I was talking to, that was the obvious reason why God would have given us Jesus.

Even simple ideas or words from the Bible can need putting in context if the pupils are going to understand the situation fully. One such example is the figure of the monarch. In the times when the Bible was written the monarch had absolute power, and performed a totally different role in society from the monarchs in Britain today. If the pupils are unaware of this, though, and think that monarchs in Old Testament times spent most of their time opening new buildings, it will affect their understanding of why monarchs did certain things. They might not understand why people then did not question the monarchy in the way people do today. Just talking about some of the things monarchs did, without explaining why, can make them seem more like characters out of fairy stories than real historical figures.

Assemblies are an opportunity to present Christianity to pupils who may otherwise never hear what the Bible has to say. When taking assemblies you have the opportunity to make sure the pupils do not grow up never having heard God's message in the Bible. But assemblies need to be handled carefully, and particularly the words and phrases that are used.

REMEMBER

- **Be careful how you describe truth.**
- **Use phrases like 'I believe that...', or 'The Bible teaches that...'.**
- **Avoid using jargon words or phrases.**
- **Explain any words the pupils might misunderstand.**

How can I use music in assemblies?

Many people's first experience of singing in a large group will have been at school. For all its faults, singing with others does have some good points which should encourage us to use it. Corporate singing can be very positive in a varied programme: individuals singing or playing; bands; tapes etc. It can build a group identity; allow all the pupils to contribute; help to focus on a particular point; provide an opportunity for physical movement; give space for individual expression and add variety. However, these benefits are often overshadowed by the questions: 'What shall we sing?' and 'How are we going to sing it?' Here are some guidelines to help you answer these questions.

Think about the words and be careful about what you are asking the pupils to sing. Songs based on objective truths about God and Jesus are inclusive to most people and useful. Songs demanding a personal response to the Gospel are exclusive, and many modern songs use jargon which is incomprehensible to non-Christians. Beware of picking songs that will cause chaos, or make everyone embarrassed, as it may put them off the person of Jesus. Encourage the pupils with their singing. If you are not embarrassed, they are less likely to be. Link the song to the theme of the assembly. If you can't find what you want, why not take a tune the pupils know and write different words to it.

Ensure that the tune is good and can be sung by boys whose voices are breaking. Many contemporary worship songs are difficult for younger teenagers to sing, and often a simpler tune will be sung better. If a tune is badly written, it will be unsatisfactory and probably unsingable. Try not to use songs that are beyond your capabilities. Make sure you can play or sing the song.

Bear in mind the culture of the pupils. Many hymns will not go down well with pupils; however, many up-beat contemporary worship songs are suitable. Try writing, or ask the pupils to write, a rap of a Psalm or other passage. Be aware of what they are listening to; you can not always match it, but you might meet it halfway.

Find out what the pupils regularly sing and use something they know. If you are introducing a song, leave a copy so that it can be sung again. Make sure the words are clear and correctly spelt. Pupils will not sing if they cannot read the words, and the school will not be pleased if you spell things incorrectly. Think beforehand whether you want to sing the song once, twice, or backwards! Whatever you do, make sure everyone is clear.

Be creative and have fun. Try using some non-embarrassing physical movements. Use taped music or get a competent Christian artist to perform an item. Try not to use the same style of music all the time, and encourage the pupils to create their own music. If they only have the piano, ask a guitarist to come and play. If you are using the school piano make sure it is in tune and usable. If it isn't, try to borrow a keyboard. If you use guitars, make sure they are in tune. If you have no musical skills you may be able to find someone who can help you.

If you have started a song and it does not work, keep going. You may have a good relationship with the school and be able to stop, but be careful before doing this. If the whole thing seems an unrewarding slog then look hard at the culture. Music is a key form of expression almost everywhere, so persevere.

In some schools music is a regular and essential part of the assembly. Sadly, many schools never have music and you might be the only person to bring some in. Done carefully, sensitively and with good preparation, it can be fantastic. For many young people, the written word conveys little meaning and music is often the medium through which they express themselves, and are able to worship God.

REMEMBER

- **Never ask pupils to sing things that are not true for them or that make little sense.**
- **Encourage the pupils with their singing.**
- **Ensure that the tune can be sung by boys whose voices are breaking.**
- **Find out what the pupils regularly sing.**
- **Try not to use the same style of music all the time.**

Josiah

The importance of the Bible

2 Chronicles 34 and 35

Aim

That the pupils would see that Christians believe the Bible is the word of God and the result this has.

Rubbish Hunt

Set up three containers each containing bits of paper of two different colours, and some sweets hidden amongst it all. Ask for three volunteers, each of whom must stand by one of the containers. They have one minute to separate out the paper, putting one colour in one pile, and the other colour in another. Tell them if they find anything else in their container, they must put that in another pile. Don't let on that there are any sweets in the container. When the minute is up tell them that they can keep any sweets they have found.

Input

In the game people had to sort through rubbish, and in the process they discovered rewards. Explain that you are going to be talking about a King who reigned in Judah in about 600BC. He discovered things in a similar way to the people playing the game.

Bible Reading

The key part is **2 Chronicles 34:19-32**. You could either read this (see **Nuts & Bolts** page 10 for ideas) or tell it in your own words. If you want to set the scene, **chapter 34:1,2,8** and **14-18** are an easy and quick way to do so.

Input

Josiah was pushing through reforms in his country and was working hard to do what was right in the eyes of the Lord. He sent his servants to repair the ruined temple. They were probably expecting to sort through the rubble and then start rebuilding. But just like the game, as they cleared away the rubbish they discovered something else. What they discovered was the Book of the Law which is the first part of what Christians call the Old Testament. Josiah realised that what it said was serious and, more importantly, he believed it was the word of God and was true.

What Do You Believe?

Read out some statements, and ask the pupils to say whether they believe them or not. Make them fairly humorous and do them in fairly quick succession. They could be things like: 'Do you believe in Father Christmas?' 'Do you believe that coming to school is the best thing ever?' The last one wants to be 'Do you believe that the hall ceiling is about to fall down?' Make the point that you could already tell that no one believed that, because if they did they wouldn't be sitting here listening to you, but would be outside away from danger.

When Josiah read the Book of the Law he believed it was true and acted on that. He repented of all the wrong he had done, and held a huge celebration to praise God for what he had done in the past. In fact, Josiah went on to base the whole of his life on the teachings from the Law.

The Bible Today

Use the information on the **Amalgam** page to show how the Bible is being taken round the world today. Highlight some of the statistics and information showing how many copies there are of the Bible. Point out that this many are made to try and meet the demand. Many people in the world want and read their Bible.

You could copy the facts and put them on an OHP so everyone can see them. You might want to leave these up for people to read as they leave the assembly.

Input

All around the world Christians have the same attitude to the Bible that Josiah had. Christians believe it is the word of God, and that Jesus said that his followers (Christians) should read the Bible and obey it. It should be the same for Christians as it was for Josiah.

BIBLE FAX

Number of Bibles in the world:

It is impossible to even estimate such a vast number. The Bible has been translated into more languages than any other book that exists!

Languages currently spoken in the world:	**6,497**
Languages with some or all of the Bible:	
All the Bible	**273**
New Testament only	**676**
New Testament translation in process	**1,209**
Total	**2,158**
Languages needing translation:	At least **1000** possibly **2000**.

Time required to translate a New Testament:

Varies depending on local circumstances. Computers and the use of native translators has made the process quicker. It now takes 10-25 years!

Cost:

Impossible to say.
You need to calculate the cost of having a translation team and their families on the job.
Costs would include: food, housing, clothing, medical care, travel, education for the children, pay for helpers, typesetting, publication, distribution and so on....
These costs need to be kept up for, perhaps, 20 years!

What people have said when they first received a translation:

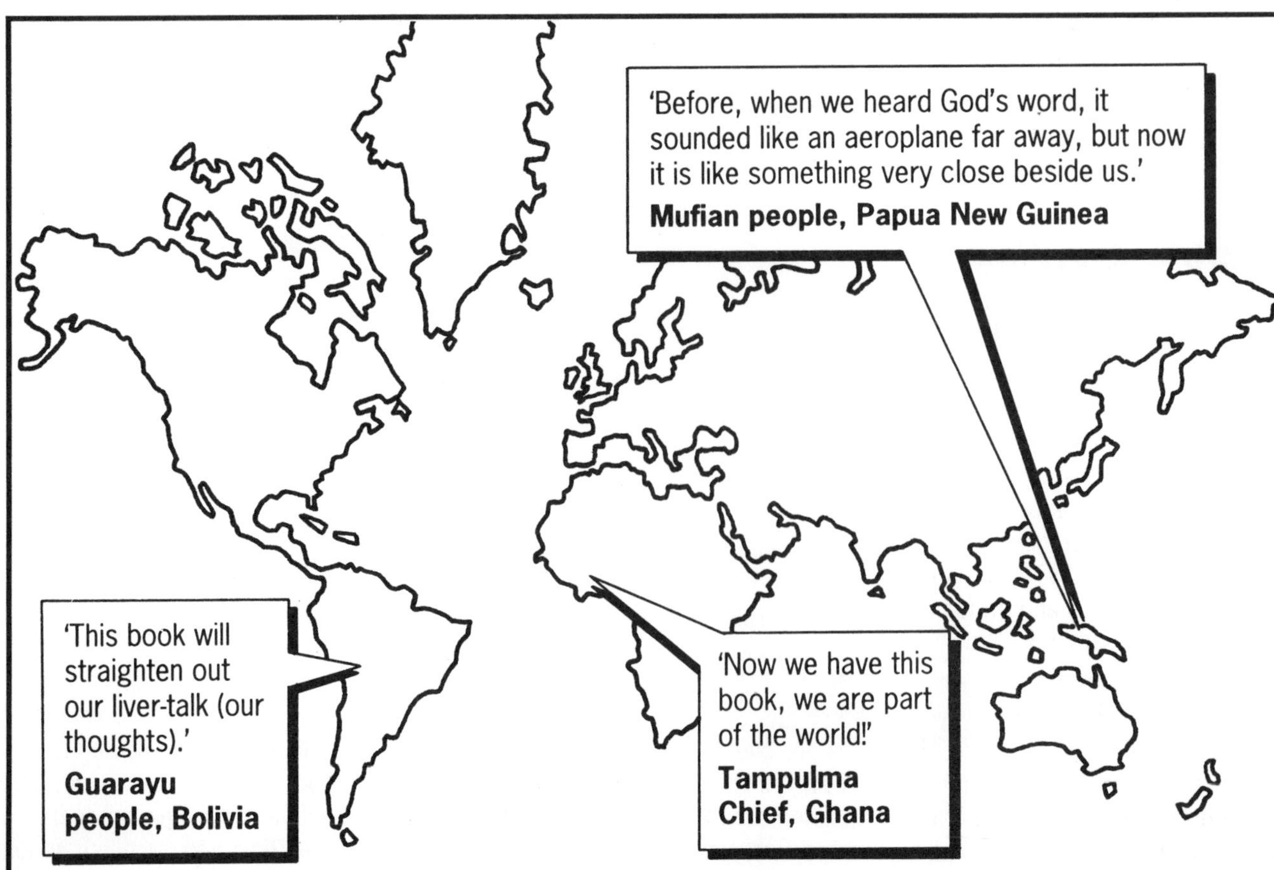

These facts were supplied by Wycliffe Bible Translators.

Elijah

Only one God

1 Kings 18

Aim

That the pupils would realise that the Bible teaches that there is only one God, and we have the choice whether to go along with that or not.

Take Your Pick

Set up the following game. Have a series of boxes (or envelopes) numbered from 1-6, and put prizes, such as sweets, in 3 of them. Ask for three volunteers and tell them that they have to choose a box, and that whichever they choose is their box. Explain that there are prizes in only three of them. When they've made their choices ask them to open the boxes and see if they've won a prize. You may need to open the others to prove it wasn't rigged!

Input

Make the point that the contestants had to choose a box and then stick to that choice. Draw out how difficult it was for them not knowing what was in the different boxes. Help everyone to see that if they knew what was in each box the choice would have been a lot easier.

Tell the Story

The story of Mount Carmel provides a great opportunity to bring the Bible alive for the pupils. You could either read it from the Bible or put it into your own words. Either way, the pictures on the **Amalgam** page can be used during the telling. If you are using an OHP you could also make some fire from heaven by making a mask of a bolt of lightning, then sticking some acetate on the mask and colouring it like fire. Put this on the OHP at the appropriate moment and flash the OHP on and off for a highly technical special effect (see **Nuts & Bolts** page 4 for extra ideas on using OHPs). Whichever way you do it, give some background information about the drought and the circumstances which led to the confrontation.

Highlight **chapter 18:21**. Just like in the game at the beginning the people had to make a choice. Elijah was fed up with the people wavering between God and Baal. It was now time to make a choice, and it was up to the people to decide who was God and who they were going to follow. Unlike the game, though, Elijah didn't want people to be just guessing who was God, he wanted them to be sure.

Totally Unique

Display the following lists one at a time and see if people can guess the connections:

A - John Major,
Margaret Thatcher,
Edward Heath,
Winston Churchill

(They have all been Prime Ministers)

B - Bryan Adams,
The Beatles,
Cilla Black,
Kraftwerk

(They've all had number 1 hit singles)

C - The Eiffel Tower,
Aston Villa Football Club,
The Moon,
You

(There is only one of each of them)

Input

Point out that in the last group each of the things is completely unique. There is only one of them. The Bible tells us that the reason Elijah went through the test on top of Mount Carmel was to establish with the people that there is only one God.

The Old Testament spends a lot of time making this point over and over again, and Christians today still believe this to be true, that there is only one God. Christians now, like the people then, have made the choice that there is only one God and that they are going to follow Him.

3
2
1

Abraham

God keeps his promises

Genesis 15 and 21

Aim

That the pupils would learn that Christians trust God because he is trustworthy and keeps his promises.

The Totally Trustworthy Test

Start by doing some trust exercises — the kind of thing where someone falls back and you catch them. Ask for one volunteer to come out and do the exercise, and promise them a prize, such as a packet of crisps, if they do it. After that person has done the exercise and won a prize, ask for another volunteer who would like to do the same thing and win another prize. You should find that people are far more willing to try this once one person has had a go. (I'm afraid I can't guarantee the pupils' response, but this usually works.)

Input

People are far more likely to trust someone who they know is reliable. People often use the same shops, buy a particular make of clothes, or use the same garage to repair their car because those people or things have proved reliable in the past. We all like to have that security so that we don't have the worry of being let down. In the Bible we can read a lot about people who are reliable and some who are decidedly unreliable, but the Bible has a great deal to say about the reliability of God.

Abraham, Sarah and Isaac

Tell the story of the promise and birth of Isaac. You could read **Genesis 15:1-6** and then **Genesis 21:1-7** as an outline of the events. You may wish to include **Genesis 17:1-10** as well. Point out that God promised Abraham a son when he was about 85 years old, but his son wasn't born until he was 100. He had to wait 15 years before God fulfilled his promise. In **Romans 4:19** there is a graphic description of Abraham's condition, and his continuing trust. Get the pupils to think what that must be like, to be promised a son when you are 85 and your wife is 75. Humanly speaking, it looks impossible, but Abraham and Sarah trusted God. But then there was the 15 years to wait for the birth. Did they ever wonder whether it was ever going to happen? Did they ever question God's timing? They must have had many questions over the years but they kept on believing and the Bible tells us that God's promise came true. But they had another promise to wait for as well. God promised Abraham that all people would be blessed by him (**Genesis 12:3b**). Christians believe that this is looking forward to Jesus, a promise which has been fulfilled but which Abraham never saw.

Election Promises

Perform the sketch from the **Amalgam** page. See **Nuts & Bolts** page 8 for ideas on how to do sketches. Highlight the different lengths of time that John and Margaret had to wait for their ice cream. Many people find it difficult to trust God when he doesn't work to our timings, but the Bible says that God will always keep his promises.

Input

Christians today trust God because they believe he has proved himself to be trustworthy. Sometimes his timing might be different from ours, so we may have to wait to see the promise fulfilled and it may not even be in our life time.

The greatest promise Christians believe God made is that Jesus will come to earth again. We can spend eternity with God if we believe in Jesus. Christians have been waiting for him to return for nearly 2000 years. It might seem stupid to go on waiting, but Christians believe that they can trust God on this matter because he has proved himself to be totally trustworthy in the past.

ELECTION PROMISES

(ENTER WILBERFORCE SLIMEBALL MP, SHOUTING HIS SPEECH AS HE ENTERS. IF THIS COULD BE DONE THROUGH A MEGAPHONE THAT WOULD BE GREAT; IF HE COULD BE RIDING A BIKE AS WELL THAT WOULD BE AMAZING! DURING THE SPEECH JOHN AND MARGARET HAGGLE AND SHOUT AT WILBERFORCE, AND ALSO THROW THINGS AT HIM. SCREWED UP PAPER IS PROBABLY EASIEST BUT OLD CABBAGES AND SOCKS WOULD LOOK GOOD.)

Wilberforce: Voters of Little Sludge Bucket under the Swamp, you have elected me, Wilberforce Slimeball, as your MP for the next 4 years. I now promise to serve you faithfully in parliament. I will support your causes. I will fight for your needs. I will **not** kiss any of your babies. I will shout 'hear, hear' when I'm on telly. I will do all these things, but the first thing I will do is give every citizen of this proud and noble slum a free ice cream! Do you hear me?

Margaret: What?

Wilberforce: Free ice cream I tell you. Free! Free! (HE EXITS STILL SHOUTING ABOUT FREE ICE CREAM.)

John: What a load of rubbish, free ice cream indeed! I've never heard anything so stupid, that guy is a fraud.

(ENTER ICE CREAM DELIVERER, THIS COULD BE WILBERFORCE WITH A DIFFERENT HAT ON.)

Ice cream deliverer: Here you are sir, free ice cream courtesy of Wilberforce Slimeball MP, BA, PhD, OBE, BC, QED, BP ETC.

John: Hey! Great! Thanks! I always said he was a great politician. (HE STARTS TO EAT.)

Margaret: No you didn't! You said he was a fraud.

John: Did I? Ah...er....well I meant... award... yes, that guy should win an award.

Margaret: Huh! Well if he's so good where's my ice cream, eh? Come on, fair's fair.

Ice cream deliverer: Well I'm afraid my box is empty. I'll go and get some more and then you can have your ice cream. (HE EXITS.)

Margaret: Oh yeah, and I suppose I just have to sit around like a lemon waiting for him to come back. I'm off!

John: Oh stop your stupid sulking. You should certainly stop scurrilously slandering Slimeball and stay. Soon super Slimeball will supply you with superior strawberry and satsuma ice cream.

Margaret: That's easy for you to say! But you've got yours.

John: Yours will be here soon.

Margaret: (SUDDENLY GETTING VERY FRIENDLY). John, John, you know how much you like me, and how we always stick together and help each other?

John: Yeeees?

Margaret: Well I was wondering if I could... Well what I mean is can I... Look, what I'm trying to say is... Oh, give us some of your ice cream!

John: No!

Margaret: Oh go on!

John: No! You wait for yours to be delivered.

Margaret: Oh don't be so mean, give me some ice cream. (SHE TRIES TO GRAB IT.)

John: No, get off! This is mine. (THEY STRUGGLE WITH THE ICE CREAM SHOUTING AT EACH OTHER. AFTER A SHORT STRUGGLE THEY DROP THE ICE CREAM – OR SQUISH IT INTO JOHN'S FACE IF YOU PREFER.)

John: Oh, now look what you've done.

Margaret: Well it serves you right, all I wanted was some ice cream.

(ENTER THE ICE CREAM DELIVERER. HE HANDS MARGARET AN ICE CREAM.)

Ice cream deliverer: Here you are, I've got your ice cream for you. (THEY ALL FREEZE.)

Paul

God's love is for everyone

Acts 9:1-8

Aim

That the pupils would learn that the Bible teaches that God loves everybody.

Person of the Year Show

Organise a Person of the Year Show with four contestants who will be the characters from the **Amalgam** page. Ask for three pupils to be judges and give them cards to hold up to vote. They each need to have one card saying 'Like', and one saying 'Dislike'. As the contestants walk on read the descriptions of each from the Amalgam page. The judges need to make their choice when you have read out the descriptions. Make a note of how the judges vote and comment on this afterwards. Point out any which got all three liking them or all three disliking them.

Input

We all have opinions about people, and what we think of them will alter how we treat them. We often form our opinions of people on just hearsay rather than taking the trouble to get to know them.

Person of the Year AD40

Ask the pupils to imagine it is AD40 and you are taking an assembly for them. Once again you are having a Person of the Year Show, but this time one of the characters is an enthusiastic young man. He is a hard working tent maker who spends his spare time persecuting Christians. He travels around hunting out all the Christians he can find and then has them tortured and killed. Explain that this is what a man called Saul was like and that in his own words he persecuted the church and tried to destroy it. (**Galatians 1:13**)

Input

Saul was a violent and undesirable person, particularly if you were a Christian. The Bible says that it was God's people, the Christians, that Saul was persecuting. The Bible says (in effect) he was persecuting Jesus (**Acts 9:5**). Many people's attitude to life is 'give as good as you get'. If Jesus had had this attitude Saul would have been in trouble. We need to be thankful that Jesus has a different set of values.

Saul's Conversion

Read the account of Saul's conversion from **Acts 9:1-8**, or retell it using your own words.

Input

Jesus did not destroy Saul, but the Bible says that Jesus told Saul to get up because he had something for him to do. The Bible goes on to say that Saul (who became known as Paul) became a follower of Jesus with as much passion as he had previously used to persecute Christians. He spent his time preaching and telling others about Jesus.

Pupils' Personal Preferences

Refer the pupils back to the people in the Person of the Year Show. Everyone will have formed an opinion about them. We could probably grade ourselves alongside them. We might think we are better than the car thief, but not as good as the brain surgeon. People like to have an opinion on where they stand in society. It is nice to think that we are not as bad as some other people.

In the days when Saul was persecuting Christians, he would have been considered by many to be one of the bad guys. Many people would have thought he deserved punishment for all the things he was doing, but after he became a Christian, the Bible says that Paul discovered something amazing about God.

Input

Paul wrote in his letter to the Christians in Rome that God demonstrated his love for people in a dramatic way. Paul said that God sent his son Jesus to be punished for our sins while we were still sinners. (**Romans 5:8**). What Paul realised was that God does not have a list of favourites. He loves everybody. Paul also said that God does not wait for us to become really nice people. He loves us anyway. This is one of the great truths that Christians believe. God loves everybody. No one is unlovable to God.

THE PERSON OF THE YEAR SHOW

Below are the four descriptions of the people used in the Person of the Year Show. Get the contestants to walk in as if on a catwalk and read out the descriptions as if it is a fashion show. Feel free to change the sexes and names of the contestants as appropriate.

Dr Fiona Symms OBE

Dr Fiona Symms is a consultant brain surgeon and works in London. She studied medicine in Birmingham and then went on to do a correspondence course in applied brain surgery. A highly respected doctor, she is most widely known for her pioneering work in brain transplant surgery and was awarded the OBE in 1987 following a successful operation to implant a canary's brain in a kangaroo. Her discoveries in the field of neurology led to her receiving the Nobel prize in 1990. She is currently researching a cure for people with bad taste in clothes.

1

Brian Jones

Brian lives in Glasgow and is married to Sonya. They have two children, a cat, eighteen gerbils and a mortgage. Having been a fork lift truck diver for much of his working life, Brian was made redundant seven years ago and has been unemployed ever since. Brian's hobbies include watching football and kicking the cat. Following a recent holiday to Scunthorpe, Brian has developed a keen interest in body building. This was sparked off after he came a close 4th in the Mr Hunk of Scunthorpe competition. His ambitions include winning the pools, becoming managing director of ICI and buying a house in Beverley Hills.

2

Babs

Babs, full name Barbara Felicity Hayes-Barton, dropped out of finishing school at the age of 18. She left the boarding school and has lived on the street ever since, preferring the rough and ready lifestyle to the confines of life with her parents at Lister Hall. Babs' early years were spent in the company of her three nannies, and she had travelled the world by the age of ten. For her thirteenth birthday she got My Little Pony. She called him Desert Orchid and later sold him to a race horse owner. Babs became fed up with the glamorous lifestyle of her youth, complaining that the servants cramped her style. She now spends much of her time stealing cars and driving them into rivers. Her proudest moment was stealing a Ferrari whilst the driver was still inside. She has also recently branched out into drug selling and is currently wanted for questioning by Thames Valley Police.

3

The Reverend Henry Huxtable

Henry Huxtable is vicar of a small church in Powys. A quiet and shy man, he enjoys the relaxed pace of life in the countryside. When not visiting old ladies or writing sermons, Henry likes to walk in the country. A keen conservationist, he spends much of his spare time helping to protect the natural environment of the earth worm, which is indigenous to Wales and is under threat of extinction. Henry trained to be a vicar in Cambridge and spent four years in Africa studying theology and East African worms. Although he only has a small congregation, he visits all of them regularly and is a popular man in the village. People in the village still talk about the 1978 Christmas concert where Henry did his impressions of earth worms round the world.

4

Cornelius

God's message is for all

Acts 10 and 11

Aim

That the pupils would learn that the Bible teaches that God does not show favouritism, but his gospel is for everybody.

School Favourites

Copy the Faveometer onto an OHP acetate. You'll need to make a needle from a thin piece of card. If you mount the Faveometer on an acetate mount you can attach the needle with a safety clip so that you can swing it from side to side. You may want to 'disguise' your OHP by having wires, plugs and other things stuck to it. You could dress up as a scientist and have your assistant Igor running round working on the OHP as you do the demonstration.

Explain that you are conducting some scientific research into young people, and you have in your possession a very sophisticated and expensive piece of apparatus that can measure human emotions. It works by picking up brainwaves coming through the air as people think about something. The more you build this up the funnier it will be when you turn the OHP on. Explain that what you want to measure today is what people's favourite food is. In a dramatic flurry, switch on the OHP and look proud of it as people snigger or groan.

For the experiment, tell the pupils that you will say the name of a food, and they have to think if it's their favourite or not. Have a list of five or six different foods, with some obvious favourites, e.g. chips; and some not so popular ones, like sprouts. As you say each one, get the pupils to think 'favourite' or 'non-favourite' and as they do this wobble the needle and move it up or down the scale keeping them guessing where it's going to stop. You can either try and guess an accurate result or do it just for laughs, i.e. make soggy cabbage winner by about 74%.

Input

Point out that we all have favourite things, whether it is food, a pop group or a certain football team. In the Bible, we read that the first Christians thought God had favourite people, but they had a lesson to learn.

God's Favourite People

Tell or read the story of Peter and Cornelius from **Acts 10**. You could do the whole of chapter 10 if you have time, or you might prefer just to focus on **verses 23b-35**. Either way, highlight **verse 34**. Peter was one of Jesus' disciples and he was one of the leaders of the first churches; he was a very important person in the early Christian Church. Yet the book of Acts tells us that he had more to learn about God. He thought that God was only really concerned with Jews and that they were God's favourite people. But this part of the Bible says that unlike us, God doesn't have favourites.

Input

The Bible says that God is not concerned with looks, abilities, age, gender or nationality, but that whoever loves God and does what is right is acceptable to him. God is concerned about what we are like inside. But he gives us all the same opportunities, and the Bible says that he wants all of us to love and obey him. Explain that just being devout and upright didn't make Cornelius a Christian, he had to go on to believe in Jesus and receive forgiveness of his sins, **verse 43**.

Christians today still believe this to be true. Christians believe that the message of Jesus is for everybody, and that God has no favourites at all. He accepts everybody. It does not matter how clever, rich, good-looking or young you may or may not be. The Bible teaches that God has the same opinion of everybody; he loves them. Why? Not because of anything that we do or are, but because he made us and wants to love us.

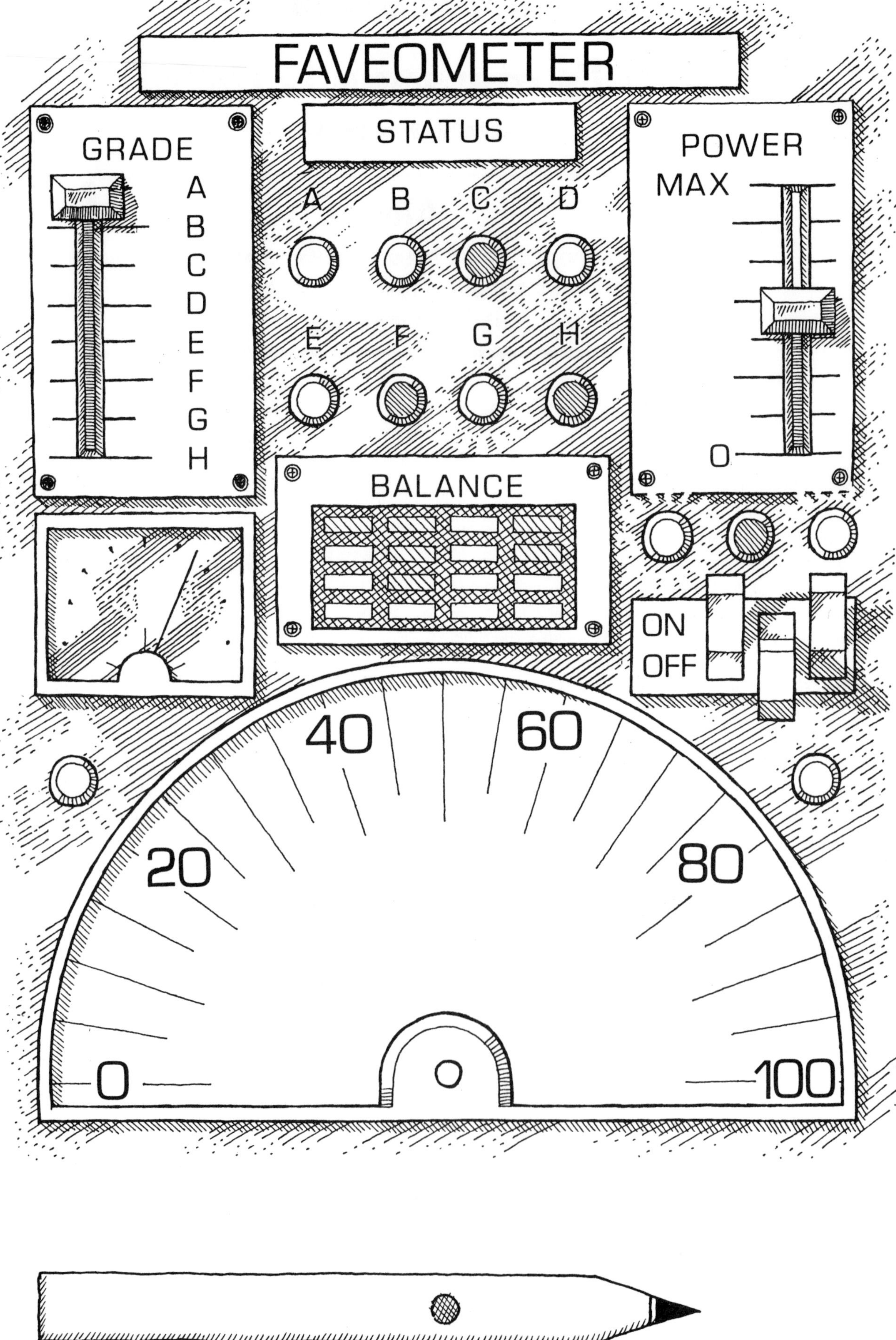
FAVEOMETER
GRADE
A
B
C
D
E
F
G
H
STATUS
A B C D
E F G H
POWER
MAX
0
BALANCE
ON
OFF
0
20
40
60
80
100

Moses

God chooses people

Exodus 1 to 4

Aim

That the pupils would learn that the Bible teaches that God's standard for choosing people is different from ours.

Hero Hour

As the pupils come into assembly, play a video of a hero (e.g. Batman or Indiana Jones). When everyone is ready, turn off the video.

Input

Explain that we all have heroes and we could all think of the person we would trust to rescue us. In the Bible there are real heroes, but God's way of choosing them is different from ours.

Choose Your Prize

This activity is brilliant, but only works once. Check that no-one else has done it in the school, or the pupils might guess the outcome.

Place a mixture of items on a tray. Have about 15, ranging from the appealing, e.g. a pound coin, to the unappealing, e.g. a Brussel Sprout. Also have a £5 note put in an envelope and then screwed up so that it looks inconspicuous. Cover the tray with a tea towel and ask for two volunteers. Build the anticipation by saying it's a chance for them to win big prizes. Explain the rules, which are: choose an object and keep it. Decide who's going first, then remove the tea towel and give them a few seconds to see everything on it. Describe what's on the tray for the other pupils and then let the volunteers choose their prize.

Input

Congratulate the volunteers on their choice, but say that although they chose well they didn't choose well enough for the star prize. Had they have chosen the screwed up envelope they would have found inside a £5 note. Produce the £5 note for all to see. The sense of disbelief and frustration has to be experienced to be believed. Point out to everyone that the volunteers chose objects based on what they could see, but it was what they couldn't see that was really worthwhile.

Moses, God's Choice.

Start the Bible input by asking if anyone knows anything about Moses. The chances are, the pupils will be able to tell you all about babies in bulrushes. Explain that Moses is a great hero of the Bible. He led six hundred thousand men plus many women and children out of slavery in Egypt (**Exodus 12:37**). The Bible says that he led those people for forty years through the wilderness, and eventually brought them to the land that God had promised them. Surely it would take a great person to do all that. Tell the pupils that you are going to find out what sort of a person Moses was. Copy the **Amalgam** page onto acetate and 'mask' the facts. As you mention each fact, uncover them until the picture is fully displayed.

1- Moses was hidden as a baby to avoid death. **Exodus 2:1-10**

2- He killed an Egyptian. **Exodus 2:11-12**

3- He ran away to avoid being caught. **Exodus 2:15**

4- He tried to wriggle out of the job God had for him. **Exodus 3:10** and **4:17**

5- He was afraid that people would ignore him. **Exodus 3:11** and **13** and **Exodus 4:1**

6- He didn't like speaking in public. **Exodus 4:10**

Input

Give the pupils time to look at what Moses was like. It doesn't seem very impressive, yet the Bible says that God chose Moses to do amazing things. Like the game where the hidden things were the best, God knew the potential that Moses had – even though Moses didn't.

Christians today still believe that God chooses people to do his work, and just like the case of Moses he doesn't always choose the rich and powerful. Those of us who follow God need to be ready for his call, whatever he asks of us.

Moses' Attributes

1.
Moses was hidden as a baby to avoid death.

2.
He killed an Egyptian.

3.
He ran away to avoid being caught.

4.
He tried to wriggle out of the job God had for him.

5.
He was afraid that people would ignore him.

6.
He didn't like speaking in public.

Mary

God's perfect plans

Luke 1:26-38

Aim

That the pupils would understand that the Bible says we should be obedient to God's plans.

This assembly is worth doing at almost any time of year except Christmas. Doing it at another time of year will help distance it from thoughts of nativity plays and traditions that people associate with this story.

Good News, Bad News

Bring in some 'junk' mail advertising big prizes that you can win. Read them out by dramatically, declaring what people can win, then add the conditions. For example, 'You can win £50,000... if you can answer 10 questions and complete a tie breaker'.

Input

All these adverts promise good news, but there are difficulties with all of them. They all require you to be able to do something.

In the Bible we read about Jesus' mother, Mary. Mary received some good news. She was promised a son, something all couples would have wanted. But there was a difficulty, because she was going to conceive him before she was married, and Joseph would not be his father. At the time, having a baby when you were not married would have meant being rejected by all your family and friends. But more than that, it could have meant the death sentence for adultery.

Mary's News

Read the account of how Mary received the news of her pregnancy from **Luke 1:26-38**. See **Nuts & Bolts** page 10 for ideas.

God's Plans

After Jesus was born, Mary and Joseph got married. They probably had all the usual festivities and parties that go with a wedding. They would have had a lot to organize. These days, weddings can also take a lot of planning. Display the picture from the **Amalgam** page and run through the list of all the things needed to prepare for a wedding in a church. When you have done that, ask if anyone can spot anything that you have not done (the answer you are looking for is: buy a wedding ring).

Input

The Bible teaches that Mary's baby was no accident. It was not even a spur of the moment thought for God. It was part of his plan, and one even more complicated than organizing a wedding. Everything needed to be in place. Mary was the last link in the chain. If she had said 'No', it would have stopped the plan, just as if you turned up to a wedding without a wedding ring.

Obedience

When you finally get to the wedding service, one of the last things you say as a single person is, 'I will'. You publicly state your agreement to take your partner as your wife or husband. This is the last chance you have to stop everything should you want to. As we have seen, the Bible says that Mary was the last part of a huge plan, a plan that had spanned thousands of years. You could refer to the Abraham assembly on page 17 if you have already done that one. For Mary, there was this cost: Did she want to have a child outside marriage and risk losing her friends and possibly her life? But the Bible says that Mary agreed to go along with the plan and carry God's Son. She was prepared to be obedient to the plan God had for her life. It would be difficult, but it would also carry great blessings. It would be even better than winning the £50,000 pounds from the Good News, Bad News activity.

The Bible teaches that God has a plan for our lives as well. It might not seem as grand as giving birth to the Son of God, but if we want to receive his blessings we need to be obedient to his plans.

WEDDING PLANS

Hire a nice car to take the bride and bridesmaids

Choose Bible readings to have during the service

Book someone to do the flowers for the church

Hire a photographer

Book the honeymoon

Ask people to be bridesmaids

Ask someone to be the best man

Get bridesmaids' dresses

Ask people to be ushers

Get a wedding dress

Get suits for the groom and best man

Make a wedding present list

Choose the music for the service

Book the reception

Get some 'going away' clothes

Write speeches for the reception

Send out invitations

Book the church

Jonah

God is in control

Jonah 1-4

Aim

That the pupils would learn that the Bible teaches that God is in control of all creation, and more importantly, salvation.

The Jonah Challenge

Start by saying that you are leading the assembly on Jonah, and you are setting yourself the 'Jonah Challenge', which is to get through the whole assembly **without** using the words whale or big fish! You could set a forfeit for yourself if you fail. During the assembly comment on how well you are doing in the challenge. If you succeed, finish the whole assembly by saying, 'Well, that's it. I've won the 'Jonah Challenge', and we have all had a whale of a time!'

Total Control

This activity needs to be done very fast with plenty of enthusiasm, so that everyone joins in.

Say that before you look at Jonah, you need the help of everyone in the room. Ask them all to stand up, then to face the back of the room. Tell them to raise one arm, then wiggle the fingers of their raised arm. Tell them to lower their arm, face you and all shout 'Hello'. Then get them to sit down silently (you can add extra commands if you wish to). Thank them for their co-operation and say it was for no real purpose but you enjoy being in control and having people do as you tell them.

Input

Get the pupils to think about what it is like to be in control and have people doing as you tell them. Think what it must be like to be in charge of thousands of people, perhaps as a general in the army, and what it must be like to have all those people doing as you tell them. Imagine the feeling of importance, power and responsibility. We can all think of people who have control: teachers, head teachers, MPs, Prime Ministers, Presidents. Some have a great deal more responsibility than others, but we look to them to be in control. The Bible has a lot to say about who is in control, and the book of Jonah gives some good answers.

Jonah the Story.

Briefly tell the story of Jonah using the pictures on the **Amalgam** page. Highlight all the different things God is shown to be in control of: The wind **Jonah 1:4**. The wha...great big wet thing! **Jonah 1:17**. The sea **Jonah 2:3**. The vine **Jonah 4 :6**. The worm **Jonah 4:7**. The scorching East wind **Jonah 4:8**.

Input

Explain that the book of Jonah shows God to be the one who makes the weather change, and plants and animals grow. This is very different from modern views on why things happen, but it is not a view restricted to the book of Jonah. Throughout the Bible it is God who is said to control the things that happen in the world. There is something even more significant that God is said to be in charge of. Jonah's prayer from inside the fis...huge slippery, blubbery thing, ends with Jonah praising God. He declares that 'Salvation comes from the Lord', **Jonah 2:9**.

The Bible says that the most important thing that God is in control of is people's destiny when they die. Salvation, in the Bible, means being saved from punishment, for life with God. The Bible says that God doesn't control people like puppets, so we are free to either accept or reject his salvation. But it goes on to say that God is in control of the consequence of our choice. What the book of Jonah says is, just as God is in control of nature, he is also in control of salvation. Christians still believe that it is God who is in control of salvation. Being a Christian is about believing what Jonah knew to be true, and deciding to accept God's salvation.

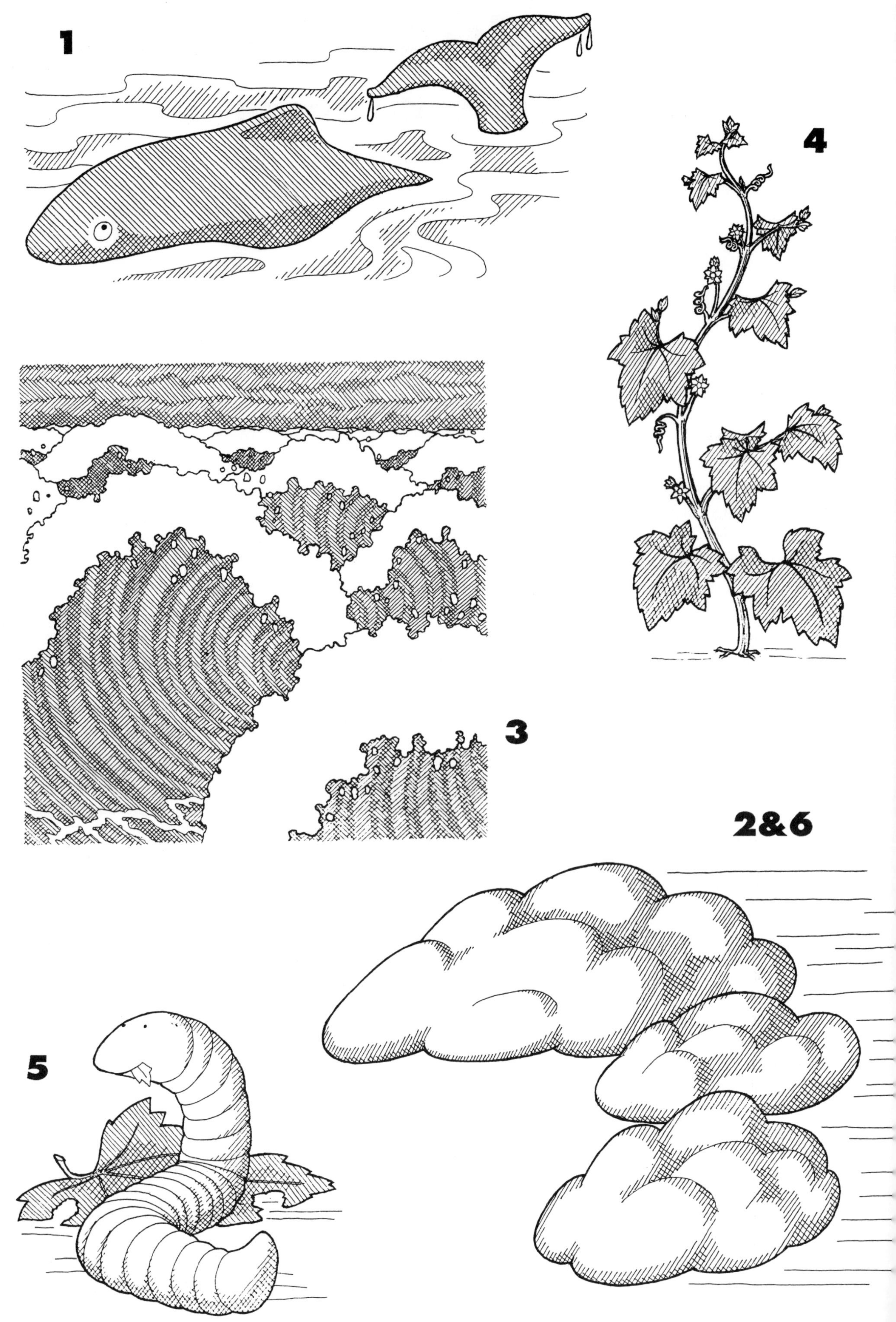
1
4
3
2&6
5

Shadrach Meshach & Abednego

God is worthy of praise

Daniel 3

Aim

That the pupils would learn that the Bible teaches that God is always worthy of praise.

Rock Idols

As the pupils enter, have some current pop music playing either on tape or a video. Leave the music playing for a short while after everyone is ready. Ask the pupils who likes, dislikes, or has been to a concert of the group you were playing.

Input

People have idols, perhaps pop stars or athletes. Some people are fanatical in their devotion to someone and spend all their money on seeing them or buying their latest albums. Sometimes the star does something wrong and people realise their devotion was misplaced. This happened to the Beatles, when on tour in America, John Lennon claimed the Beatles were 'More famous than Jesus.' This caused a public outcry and many people burned their Beatles albums in protest. In the Bible we read of many people worshipping different things. In one famous case the person realised he was worshipping the wrong thing.

No Choice

Ask everyone to stand up and face you. Tell everyone that you want them to try and touch their toes three times. When they have done this say how good it was to see them all bowing down to you giving you the respect you deserve. When the groans have subsided ask them all to sit down again.

Input

What the pupils did was not respect or bowing because they had no choice in the matter and were conned into it. In the Bible we read about a King called Nebuchadnezzar. He built a statue for people to worship, but what happened was not worship because, just like the pupils, they had no choice. If they did not worship the statue they were thrown into a fire.

Shadrach and Co.

Use the pictures from the **Amalgam** page to illustrate the following outline of events.

The Bible goes on to say that Shadrach, Meshach and Abednego refused to worship the King's statue, so they were arrested. Nebuchadnezzar told them to worship the statue or they would be thrown in the fire. They replied by saying that they did not need to defend themselves because the God they worshipped was capable of saving them. But even if he chose not to, they would still worship him because they believed he was God and not the statue that Nebuchadnezzar had built. They were duly thrown in the fire, but the Bible says they did not get burnt. In fact, when the king looked, he saw four people walking around in the fire. The fourth looked like a son of the gods. The three were brought out of the fire and Nebuchadnezzar realised that he had been worshipping the wrong thing.

Input

The Bible says that Shadrach, Meshach and Abednego worshipped God. They carried on worshipping him because they believed he was worthy of praise. Whatever happened, they were not going to praise anyone else, because no one else was worthy of their praise. Nebuchadnezzar, like some Beatles fans, realised he was worshipping the wrong thing.

The Bible says that God is worthy of praise whatever happens. We might not understand why he does some things, but he is still worthy of praise. Christians worship God for this reason. They believe that worshipping him will not turn out to be a mistake.

1
2
3

Job

Difficult questions and God's supremacy

Aim

That the pupils would learn that the Bible teaches that suffering is not linked to doing wrong, but rather suffering comes under God's plan.

Headlines

Copy 6 newspaper headlines onto acetate and cover over one word from each headline. Split the pupils into two teams and have a competition where they have to guess the missing words.

Input

Many news stories are bad news and sometimes we blame God for what is happening. The book of Job in the Bible is an apparent case of unfair suffering, but Job's response is different.

The Story of Job

Use the pictures from the **Amalgam** page to illustrate the story. Introduce Job from **Job 1:1-3**. Use the outline below to describe the encounter between Satan and the Lord. Emphasize the fact that God is in control and there is no sense of equality at all.

The angels were presenting themselves before the Lord when Satan turned up. The Lord saw Satan and asked him, 'What have you been up to?'. 'I've been wandering around on the earth,' replied Satan. 'Did you see Job when you were there?' asked the Lord. 'I tell you, there is no one like him; he never does anything wrong and he fears God.' Satan said, 'That's not surprising, is it? You've given him everything, but if you take away all that he'll curse you.' The Lord then gave Satan permission to take away everything Job had. But Job didn't curse God. He continued to praise him. So Satan said, 'OK, he still praises you. But make him ill and then you'll see his faith will vanish.' God gave Satan permission to hurt Job. Job was then covered in sores and he went and scratched his skin with some broken pottery.

The rest of the book is about Job trying to understand what has happened to him, and his friends offering suggestions. Highlight Job's despair from **Job 3:3**. The arguments from Job's friends all seem to make sense. They say that people suffer because they have been evil, and God is just. Therefore, Job must have done something wrong to be punished. Read some verses to show the friends' arguments. For example **chapter 4:7, chapter 5:17, chapter 8:3-5, chapter 11:14 and 15, chapter 34:10-12**. Throughout all this, Job questions them, as he believes he has lived a righteous life. But Job longs for God to end his suffering. Eventually the Lord answers Job, but it is not the kind of answer we would expect. Read **chapter 38**, or a part of it. (See **Nuts & Bolts** page 10 for ideas). After God's reply, Job realises how inadequate he is before God and how he spoke of things he did not know. God then restores Job and all his possessions twice over, but rebukes Job's friends because they did not speak what was right.

Input

The Bible says that Job got it right when he refused to curse God or try to understand God in simple terms. Job learnt not to blame or question God but to trust him, because Job would never be clever enough to understand him. Job went from being rich and successful, to losing everything and suffering. It seemed really unfair.

According to the Bible only one person has exceeded Job in this way. The Bible says that Jesus was perfect, but he suffered and lost everything, including his life, the ultimate unfairness. But the Bible says he rose again because Jesus was obedient to God's plan and trusted and obeyed rather than accused and rejected God.

The Bible teaches that we will never understand God until we die. Only in heaven will we understand why God allows some things to happen. God explains why we do not understand everything in Isaiah 55:8 and 9.

1
2
3

Noah

God hates sin and punishes it

Genesis 6-8

Aim

That the pupils would learn that the Bible teaches that God hates sin and has to punish it.

Introduction

Explain to everyone that you are going to be talking today about Noah, but it's not going to be about animals going into the ark two-by-two. Instead, we are going to find out why it was that God decided to destroy everything on earth apart from a few people and animals.

Book Spoiling

Have an old book that you don't mind ruining. Put the book on a table along with a glass of coke. Tell everyone what an ancient, valuable book it is. Start to cough at this point, put the book down and have a drink of coke. When you've finished drinking, go to pick the book up but knock the glass of coke so that it soaks the book. React to this disaster in a suitable fashion. As you are recovering from the shock, show everyone how the coke has spoilt the whole book as it has seeped through the pages. All you can do is throw the book away.

Evil People

The evil of mankind is described in **chapter 6:5-7**, and God declares that it needs punishing. The people who needed punishing were evil, but they wouldn't have been any more evil than us. Some were murderers or thieves, but probably, many just got into fights, or were just selfish and greedy. Like the book that got spoilt by the coke, the people were spoilt by their evil deeds. The Bible says that God hated all the wrong things the people were doing.

The Truth

Have the sketch from the **Amalgam** page performed, or lead straight into the input.

Input

Everybody has a sense of what is fair. If someone does something wrong, it's them who should be punished and not someone else. The Bible teaches that God, too, thinks that wrong-doing deserves punishment. But the Bible also teaches that God is perfectly fair, so he always gets it right. When God saw all the people on earth being evil, he had to punish them, or they would have been just getting away with it all. The book that got spoilt was destroyed. God decided that the people who were spoilt should also be destroyed.

So why did God save Noah? **Chapter 6** says Noah was righteous and blameless among the people. Note he was not blameless before God but amongst the other people. He was not perfect but was trying to live as God wanted him to. He was righteous – right with God. God also saved Noah because he wanted to save people. Why? Because, despite their disobedience, the Bible says that God loves them. So Noah and his family built the ark, put all the animals in it, and off they sailed. Most people know that it rained for forty days and nights, but they were in the ark a lot longer while the waters subsided. They were actually in the ark over a year! Imagine what that must have been like. Shut up with your family and a lot of smelly animals for over a year!

After the flood God promised never to destroy the earth again. He wasn't under the mistaken idea that we were all going to be good. (**Chapter 8:21**.) The Bible says that he knew that people would still be evil, but he wasn't going to destroy everything again. People were to learn from what he had done, and he had another plan.

In the account of Noah, God killed everybody but saved just eight people. Thousands of years later, the Bible says that the opposite happened. One person was killed to save everybody. He was Jesus Christ.

THE TRUTH!

The head teacher and Frotock can be of either sex. You may wish to add a few 'sirs' or 'madams' at appropriate places.

(THE HEAD TEACHER IS SITTING AT A DESK WRITING, THERE IS A KNOCK AT THE DOOR)

Head: Enter!

(ENTER FROTOCK)

Head: Ah Frotock, just the person I was wanting to see.

Frotock: Were you?

Head: Yes, and I am sure you know what it's all about, don't you?

Frotock: Ermm, no I don't actually. Oh! It isn't to do with the 5 broken computers and the semolina is it?

Head: The what!? No it isn't, but we'll sort that out later. No the reason I've called you here is to find out what happened yesterday lunch time when the chemistry lab exploded, taking Mr Jenkins's eyebrows, shins and armpits with it.

Frotock: (STANDING UP WITH HAND ON HEART) I can honestly say that it was nothing to do with me.

Head: Oh sit down you fool. There is good reason to suspect that you were involved. But, because this is a fair school, we will hear your side of the story.

Frotock: Well all I know is that when I was working hard in the library doing a bit of reading on the socio-political implications for the Latvian farmers following the EEC directives on farm trade subsidies as agreed under the auspices of the GATT Trade agreements in conjunction with United Nations directives which spell out the...

Head: Yes, yes get on with it. (ASIDE) What a creep.

Frotock: Well I gazed out of the window (THIS NEXT PART IS ACTED OUT BY CLIMBING ON CHAIRS, DESKS, ETC.) to see two ruffian types climb onto the roof of the art rooms, then they leapt onto the science block where they opened a skylight. After a moment's pause they threw something into the block, and I didn't see anything else after that.

Head: Why not?

Frotock: Because the wall of the library landed on my desk due to the force of the explosion.

Head: I don't wish to doubt you Frotock, but you're lying, aren't you?

Frotock: No,no,no,no,no,no,no,no,no,no,no,no,no. I'm innocent. Honestly, how could you think such a thing?

Head: (RISING SLOWLY AND SELECTING A GOOD CANE) Because, Frotock, I saw you do it.

Frotock: (REALISING THEY HAVE BEEN CAUGHT) Ah!

(THEY BOTH FREEZE)

Belshazzar

Don't ignore God's warnings

Daniel 5

Aim

That the pupils would learn that the Bible teaches that God gives us warnings that he expects us to heed.

Setting the Scene

This event happens on the eve of the collapse of the Babylonian empire. The King Belshazzar was ignoring the threat of the new empire of the Medes and Persians. With their armies marching on Babylon, Belshazzar threw a party to try and show his strength and lack of concern at the events that were unfolding around him.

Belshazzar's Party

Have a bag containing all the things one needs for a party. For example, some crisps, a can of coke, some party poppers, etc. At the bottom of the bag have some more impressive looking cups. If you are able, take a communion cup to show the kind of vessel that may have been taken from the temple. As you describe the party (using the outline below) bring out the various props. Stop the story occassionally to eat and drink, and offer some to the pupils. The more you build the party the greater the contrast will be when you bring out the communion cup.

Belshazzar was throwing a party. He had done all the usual things people do to get ready for a party and everything was going well. Drink was drunk, people were drunk and the food was scoffed. People let off their party poppers without a care in the world and danced all night. When the party was in full swing, Belshazzar decided to show how brave and powerful he was. By ignoring all the traditions and superstitions, he was going to get the drinking vessels from the temple and drink from those. So the vessels were fetched and everyone drank from them and laughed at the superstitions of the Israelites and praised their own gods of metal, wood and stone.

But suddenly, the King screamed out in fear, because he could see a large hand writing something on the wall (use the picture from the **Amalgam** page). He called for all his advisors to tell him what it meant, but none of them had a clue. Eventually Daniel was called for. He was able to tell what the writing meant. Belshazzar's grandfather, Nebuchadnezzar, had been a powerful king, but he had become proud. So God had taken away his throne.

For seven years he had been insane, living in the fields, until he recognised that God was sovereign over the kingdoms. Daniel told Belshazzar that he should have learned that lesson. The words were 'MENE, MENE, TEKEL, PARSIN', and they meant 'Numbered, Numbered, Weighed, Divided'. Belshazzar's days were **numbered** because he had failed to learn the lessons from his grandfather. He had been **weighed** in the balance of right and wrong and had been found wanting and so the Kingdom was going to be taken and **divided** between the Medes and the Persians. The Bible says, that on that night, Darius the Mede killed Belshazzar and overthrew the Babylonian empire.

Input

Christians believe that the lessons in the Bible are as relevant today as they were when the Bible was written. The Bible gives lots of teaching about God's power and sovereignty, and warnings about what happens if people ignore those warnings. Some people don't like to think of God getting angry or giving people guidelines by which to live, but the Bible says that is what he does. Christians believe that God still gets angry with people who ignore his warnings – not that he zaps people when they do something naughty, but that he knows everything that we do. Belshazzar went wrong because, even though he knew what God was like, he did nothing about it. Christians believe that when we do things wrong, if we are truly sorry and promise to obey God in future, he will always forgive us. So we don't have to be fearful of punishment from him.

MENE MENE
TEKEL
PARSIN

Achan

The consequences of sin

Joshua 7 and 8:1-29

Aim

That the pupils would learn that the Bible teaches that sin always has consequences, and that God takes it seriously.

Major Apologize

Have the sketch from **Amalgam** performed. At the end, point out the consequence of Beryl and Brian's action. Often we do things without thinking what the consequences might be.

Coke Consequences

Before the assembly, 'doctor' a can of coke by piercing a couple of holes in the bottom and emptying out the contents. Refill the can with water and plug the holes with some blu-tak. During your introduction shake the can whilst you are talking.

Introduce the assembly by saying that you are going to be thinking about consequences. Some consequences are obvious: if we eat too much we will be sick; if we win all our matches, our team will be the champions; and if I open this can over the people in the front row... (open the can towards them). Point out that some consequences are different from what we expect. In the Bible we read about Achan, who found this to be true.

Tell The Story

If you are doing an assembly with younger pupils, 6th or 7th year, you might want to tell the story using the Blood and Honey video featuring Tony Robinson. The video is called Judges volume 1 and the story of Achan is called 'Joshua in Trouble Valley'. For details of how to get the video see **Nuts & Bolts** page 63.

If you are not going to be using the video, set the scene by saying that Joshua had just led the Israelite army in a famous victory over the city of Jericho. They had destroyed the city and had been commanded by God to leave all the treasure they found in the city to be destroyed (this is in **chapter 6:17-19**). But we are told at the start of **chapter 7** that Achan disobeyed God and took some of the treasure, and this made God angry. The next city the Israelites attacked was Ai, a small town, which should have been easy for the Israelites to take. But the men of Ai routed the Israelites and defeated them.

That night, as Joshua prayed to God, the Bible says that God told Joshua that someone had disobeyed him, which is why they were defeated at Ai. If they wanted God to give them victory, they had to punish the thief.

The next day everyone was lined up, and the priests, directed by God, called people out until they came to Achan. He confessed that he had seen the treasure and had stolen some and hidden it. The people found the treasure and stoned Achan and his family to death. Then the Israelites went and captured Ai.

Input

Achan probably thought he would get away with stealing some of the treasure. Who would know? The people of Jericho had been killed so why shouldn't he have it? It wasn't as if it was going to affect anyone else. But this was not so. The Bible teaches that God knows all that we do, and that all sin has consequences. Achan's sin led to the defeat of the Israelites and the death of him and his family. This might seem harsh, but it is a vivid demonstration of the seriousness of sin in God's sight.

All of us do things wrong, sometimes accidently, sometimes deliberately. We need to think what the consequences of our actions are going to be. We might not think there have been any, but the Bible says that they do have consequences. Our actions affect other people and also ourselves.

One of the worst consequences for Achan was that he angered God. The Bible says that even today when we do things wrong, one of the consequences is that we make God angry and cut ourselves off from him.

MAJOR APOLOGIZE

THERE IS A FRISBEE ON STAGE.

ENTER BERYL AND BRIAN.

Brian: Hey Beryl, look! Someone's left a Frisbee lying around.

Beryl: Where?

Brian: Here. Look! (HE KICKS IT.)

Beryl: Oooooh yes.

Brian: It's quite a good one, isn't it?

Beryl: Oooooh yes.

Brian: It's a bit odd it lying around out here in the middle of nowhere, isn't it?

Beryl: Oooooh yes.

Brian: Oh shut up! Look, shall we have a go with the Frisbee?

Beryl: Oooooh no.

Brian: What?

Beryl: Oooooh no.

Brian: Why not?

Beryl: Well, it probably belongs to someone.

Brian: Who? There are no humans around for miles. (THEY BOTH PEER INTENTLY AT THE PUPILS.)

Beryl: Yeah! You're right. No one could have thrown it this far.

Brian: Come on then. (HE PICKS THE FRISBEE UP AND THROWS IT TO BERYL, THEY THROW IT TO EACH OTHER A FEW TIMES, CONGRATULATING EACH OTHER, CHEERING AS THEY CATCH IT ETC. AFTER A FEW THROWS BRIAN THROWS IT QUITE HARD AND IT GOES OUT OF SIGHT.)

Beryl: Oh! You've lost it now.

Brian: Yeah! But it was a good throw. Look, it's landed on the roof of that big building.

Beryl: Oh yeah. (THEY ARE STILL PEERING TOWARDS THE FRISBEE WHEN MAJOR APOLOGIZE ENTERS BEHIND THEM AND STARTS LOOKING AROUND.)

Major Apologize: Excuse me. (BERYL AND BRIAN ARE BOTH STARTLED.)

Brian: Can we help you?

Major Apologize: I'm Major Apologize from the 14th Foot, Eye and Ear regiment.

Beryl: Sorry?

Major Apologize: I'm Major Apologize

Brian: Sorry?

Major Apologize: I'm Major Apologize. Look, will you stop all this nonsense and assist me in military manoeuvres.

Beryl: Certainly. How can we help you?

Major Apologize: I'm looking for a large yellow (OR WHATEVER COLOUR YOUR FRISBEE IS) disk that should be on the ground around here somewhere. Have either of you seen it?

Beryl: Well...

Brian: No!

Major Apologize: Oh well, I shall continue my search.

Beryl: Um, was it anything important?

Major Apologize: Important? It's a target for the RAF 47th squadron. They are testing their new XXX bomb today and it will be programmed to hit that target.

(BERYL AND BRIAN LOOK IN HORROR TOWARDS WHERE THE FRISBEE WENT. MAJOR APOLOGIZE LOOKS ANGRILY AT THEM. THEY ALL FREEZE.)

Naaman

The danger of pride

2 Kings 5:1-16

Aim

That the pupils would learn that pride can get in the way of all sorts of blessings, and can prevent us from receiving what God wants to give us.

Dog Food Breakfast

Prepare a dog food tin in the following way. Undo a tin at the bottom and empty out the contents. Wash and clean the inside of the tin. Refill with chocolate mousse and chopped up Milky Way and freeze until solid. Stick the bottom of the tin back on with Sellotape. Allow to thaw partly before the assembly. 45 minutes is usually about right. Test this the day before to know how long to thaw it, so you get that authentic dog food texture.

At the start of the assembly apologize for the fact that you have not had any breakfast yet. Explain that you really can't take an assembly on an empty stomach, so you will have to have something to eat. Produce the tin of dog food, a tin opener and a fork. Open the tin from the top and start to eat, making sure everyone can see what it is you are eating. Offer it around to see if anybody would like some. Try to persuade them how nice it tastes.

Input

Explain that actually it is not dog food but chocolate, as any who have tried it will confirm. But to find this out, people had to be prepared to try eating something which might seem repulsive to us.

Bible Reading

Either read or tell the story of Naaman from **2 Kings 5:1-16**. Point out what the river Jordan was like, a small rather dirty little river, not much more than a large stream.

Input

Naaman was the commander of an army and was used to dignity and power. To wash in a small dirty river was degrading and repulsive. But if he hadn't washed in it he would not have been healed. It was the same with the tin of dog food. To eat it might have seemed repulsive, but it was only when you did, that you discovered the benefits. Part of Naaman's problem was his pride. He thought that washing in a dirty river was beneath him. It may be that he would have preferred to have had to bring back 10 of his enemies tied together. This would have proved he deserved to be healed, but how stupid it would have been if he had refused to wash and so had not been healed! It is easy for us to see how crazy that would be when we look back at it. We probably think that we would never do a thing like that. But do we?

Water Way To Go!

Have the sketch from the **Amalgam** page performed. See **Nuts & Bolts** page 8 for ideas.

Input

The Bible teaches that we are all proud, and we can probably think of times when we have been too proud to admit our mistakes or apologize.

For Naaman, being proud nearly cost him his health and possibly his life. When we are proud it may well be that we are missing out on a good thing, but the Bible says there is one important thing that we can miss out on by being too proud.

The Bible teaches that if we want God to forgive us for the wrong things we have done, and to accept his gift of eternal life, we must be prepared to put Jesus first in our lives. This is not easy, and many people find that their pride stops them doing this. But the Bible also teaches of the benefits of doing just that. Just like Naaman and the activity with the dog food, we can't experience the good things until we are prepared to give it a try.

WATER WAY TO GO

DAVID IS CROUCHED LOW ON THE GROUND HOLDING A LARGE PIECE OF CARDBOARD OVER HIS HEAD. HE IS LOOKING NERVOUSLY AROUND. ENTER ALBERT, DRESSED QUITE SMARTLY. HE WALKS OVER TO DAVID AND SNEERS AT HIM. DO CHANGE THE NAMES IF YOU HAVE FEMALE CAST.

Albert: What are you doing down there David, you ridiculous little fool?

David: I'm keeping out of the way, Albert. You ought to do the same as well.

Albert: Oh, don't be so ridiculous, I'm not going to start crouching around under bits of cardboard. What will people think of me?

David: They'll think you're stupid if you stand there like that.

Albert: How dare you call me stupid? (HE PUSHES DAVID OVER)

David: Oh get off, you stuck up nerd. You think you're so clever, don't you, stood there like that, all smart and posh. But you're going to regret it. If you had half a brain you would be down here sheltering like I am.

Albert: Oh well, aren't we grown up? If you want to lower yourself to insults, that's your problem. But I shall stand here as long as I want. Honestly, look at you grubbing around like some kind of aardvark. If you think I'm going to ruin these clothes by lying around in the dirt you have got another think coming. Just suppose someone I knew saw me – I would die of embarrassment.

David: Well suit yourself, but you'll get it if you just stand there.

Albert: Will you stop telling me what to do? I have no intention of disgracing myself by sitting under a box, so just lay off, OK?

David: OK! OK! Relax will yer? I was only trying to help, but if you're too stuck up to accept it, then that's your problem.

Albert: I am not stuck up. I just don't see why I should have to humiliate myself in public, that's all.

David: Well if this is humiliation, I'm happy. It's better than the alternative anyway.

Albert: Which is?

(AT THIS POINT SOME WATER IS THROWN INTO ALBERT'S FACE. THE IMPORTANT THING IS THAT HE GETS WET AND DAVID DOESN'T)

David: (GETTING UP AND COMING OUT FROM UNDER HIS CARDBOARD) The alternative to grubbing around like an aardvark is to stand around like a pilchard.

Albert: You little.............! (ALBERT CHASES DAVID OFF STAGE VERY ANGRILY)

Peter

Mistakes can be forgiven

John 18:15-18 and 25-27. John 21:15-19

Aim

That the pupils would learn that the Bible teaches that God's forgiveness is always available when we are genuinely sorry.

True Confessions

Read out the true confessions on the **Amalgam** page, and after each one ask the pupils to vote on whether they would forgive the person or not.

Input

All of us do things wrong. Sometimes we are caught out, other times we get away with it. Often people feel the need to confess and receive forgiveness for what they have done. We like to have our consciences cleared so that we can stop feeling guilty. But when we confess to people, we can never be too sure that they will forgive us. Perhaps they think we have done something unforgivable. The Bible has a lot to say about forgiveness, and one person who experienced this was Peter.

Peter's Confession

Either ask someone to read Peter's confession using the following outline, or read it straight from **John 18:15-18** and **25-27**. Ask the pupils if they think Peter should be forgiven.

'I'm Peter and I've got a confession. It's all to do with Jesus. I was one of his disciples for three years. Recently people have been wanting to arrest and kill Jesus. Somehow Jesus knew what was happening, because recently he said I would deny I ever knew him. I thought Jesus was joking, me deny him? Later Jesus was betrayed and arrested. I followed him and as I waited a girl said 'You're not one of his disciples are you?' I don't know what came over me. For some reason I said 'No'. Later some other servants asked me, 'You're not one of his disciples are you?' Now there were quite a few servants and I panicked and said 'No' again. Then someone else said he had seen me with Jesus. By now I was scared. These servants would hand me over to the guards as well. I denied ever having heard of Jesus.

Then I remembered what Jesus had said. There he was, having been arrested. He was going to be flogged and killed. It's the time when a guy needs his friends around him, and what did I do? I denied ever having known him.'

Input

This looks like a terrible thing that Peter did. He denied Jesus at his very hour of need. What would we think of someone who did that to us? But that is not the end of this part of the story. The Bible teaches that after Jesus had died he was raised to life, and when he met Peter the situation was resolved.

A Happy Ending?

John 21:15-19 is the point where Jesus confronts Peter. But he doesn't accuse him of betrayal, and he doesn't ignore him. Instead he asks Peter if he loves him. Peter's love is that for a friend, particularly a friend who has forgiven you for something you have done to them. The Bible says that Jesus not only forgave Peter, but in fact made him one of the main people to lead the church when Jesus had returned to heaven.

Input

The Bible says that Peter was forgiven by Jesus. The Bible also says that Jesus always forgives those who are genuinely sorry. We might do bad things, but the Bible says that we can never do anything so bad that we can't be forgiven. God isn't fickle like people are when we ask for forgiveness. If we are truly sorry we can always be forgiven by him.

TRUE CONFESSIONS

Ruth, an administrator.

❝ I was sitting in an armchair at home doing some homework when I managed to get some ink on the armchair. Knowing how cross this would make my mother I panicked and tried to find a solution to the problem. Just then, my younger brother came into the room and an evil idea flashed across my mind. Knowing how much he enjoys drawing, I said that I would let him come and sit on the armchair and draw. Not only that, but being a generous soul I would let him use my pen and paper as well. He gratefully accepted the offer and started work on a new masterpiece. He had not been at it long when my mother came into the room. She saw him drawing, and then saw the ink on the armchair. Coming to the only obvious conclusion, she gave him a right telling off for spoiling the beautiful armchair.❞

Ruth would like forgiveness from her brother for landing him in trouble.

Graeme, a teacher.

❝ I was on a well earned holiday from teaching, and was staying in a small village with some friends. One evening we were strolling through the village when we saw a brand new adventure playground. It had all the best things to play on: swings, seesaws and a death slide. Seeing the potential fun to be had from larking around on these new facilities, I ran across the road. I was temporarily set back by finding that the gate was at the far end of the field. Not wishing to be deterred, I climbed a small but sturdy looking fence. I had just stepped on to the top bar of this attractive wooden fence, when the bar gave way underneath my weight and I came crashing to the ground in a very undignified manner. I had managed to break the new fence around the village's new adventure playground.❞

Graeme would like forgiveness from the villagers who had to replace the new fence.

Chris, a vicar.

❝ We had a maths teacher nicknamed 'Bruno'. One day I arrived at a maths lesson before he did, and I saw one of my class mates struggling to open the door. I immediately assumed that a couple of jokers on the inside were trying to keep him out. I silently signalled to him to stand aside so that I could charge the door. He did; and I did. The next thing I was aware of was sledging across the front of the room on the top of the door. My classmate had been struggling to open the door because it was only on one hinge, which I effectively removed with my charge. After the mirth had died down I put the door carefully back in its place so that when 'Bruno' arrived...!❞

Chris would like forgiveness from the school for breaking the door down.

Martha

God's priorities

Luke 10:38-42

Aim

That the pupils would learn that God's priority for our lives is that we should receive eternal life.

Personal Preferences

For this game you will need a selection of objects that you can display in pairs. The pupils then vote for which of the two they would rather have. You will need to have some which may appear obvious to them, e.g. a can opener and a video game; some where the objects are similar, e.g. an A-Z and a novel; and some where there isn't much difference, e.g. two different music magazines. Whichever object gets the most votes should be put to one side. When you have been through all the pairs, quickly go through the ones they rejected and point out times when they would have been the best choice. For example an A-Z is more useful than a novel if you are lost.

Input

We all make choices about things. We decide which things we prefer or which things will be more useful to us. But our choices will vary depending on our needs or situation. There would be no point having a novel if we could not read. What we choose gives a clue to our priorities in life. We tend to choose things that we think are fun or important. It is the same when we choose things to do.

Going to a disco may be more fun than homework, but if we want to pass our exams we will choose to stay in and revise. Mary and Martha were two sisters who lived at the time of Jesus. The Bible teaches us about God's priorities by telling us about an event in the sisters' lives.

Mary and Martha

Use the pictures from the **Amalgam** page to tell the story of Mary and Martha from **Luke 10:38-42**, but stop the story before Jesus' answer in **verse 41**. Ask the pupils what they think Jesus should say. Get them to imagine that they are in Jesus' position. What would they say to Martha? When you have had some answers read out what Jesus' answer was.

Vital or Non-vital

Refer back to the objects from the start of the assembly. Point out that some of them are things we like, whereas some are things we would say are vital, such as a tin opener or some food. In the situation with Mary and Martha, Jesus made the distinction about choosing vital or non-vital things.

Input

Jesus said that Mary had chosen what was better. What she had chosen to do was to listen to Jesus rather than do housework. Jesus taught that the most important thing people could do was to listen to his teaching and to obey it. The Bible teaches that if we listen to Jesus' teaching and obey it, it leads to us having a right relationship with God and eternal life. The Bible describes eternal life as life in heaven when we die, and also a quality of life here and now. In the Bible we read that God created people and knows the best way for them to live. Jesus taught us that way. This was why Jesus said that Mary was choosing the better thing. She was learning how God wanted her to live.

Our Priorities for Life

We will all have to make different decisions in our lives: some fairly trivial like the ones made at the start of the assembly; some very important, like what subjects to study, which exams to take, who to marry. We will make these decisions depending on our priorities. Christians are people who follow the example of Mary and make it their main priority to learn and obey the teaching of Jesus. The Bible says that this is the most important decision we can make.

1

2

3

Rahab

Faith in action

Joshua 2. Joshua 6:24 and 25

Aim

That the pupils would learn that if we have a faith in God, we need to put it into action.

Reputations

Collect a series of photos of famous people: pop stars, athletes, politicians, etc. Display them so that the pupils can see them as they enter. Start the assembly by drawing the pupils' attention to the pictures. You could do a vote to find out which is the most popular person, or the one they would most like to have living next door.

Input

We have opinions of some people even though we've never met them, but we form opinions about them because they have got different reputations. Some people's reputations make them very appealing, while others have got such bad reputations that we wouldn't want to go near them. When Joshua and the Israelites attacked Jericho, everyone in the city was killed except Rahab and her family. Rahab had a reputation, probably quite a well known reputation because she was a prostitute.

The Spies and the Prostitute

The events from **chapter 2** are almost certain to be of interest to the pupils. Words like spies and prostitutes are always good attention getters. Tell the pupils how Joshua was planning to attack Jericho and so had sent two spies to the city to check things out. The spies decided to stay with Rahab the prostitute while they were in town. They probably thought it would be a good place to stay. In a house of ill repute, people would be used to strange men going in and out of the house and would not notice two foreigners being around.

They were unlucky. They were spotted. But Rahab helped them and she had good reason for doing so. Read **chapter 2:9-11** for Rahab's reason. The Bible says that Rahab acted because of the reputation of God. We read that she knew of the strength of God and the way he had helped the people of Israel, and she was afraid because she believed God's reputation to be true. She had faith that he could carry out his plans.

Rahab then put the faith that she had into action. She didn't just say that she believed God, she did something about it. She hid the spies so they wouldn't get caught and then helped them escape. It was because of her faith she and her family were spared when the city was destroyed.

Faith and Action

Give the pupils an example of someone today who is putting their faith into action. You may know someone you could interview in the assembly, otherwise read Joe's account of the work that he did in Glasgow. If you can, photocopy the photo onto acetate and display this as you read his account. Joe is just one person who decided to put his faith into action. Many others are doing the same all over the world. Remember, the Bible does not make actions an optional part of Christianity.

Input

What Rahab did probably did not seem very important at the time, but this event is referred to twice in the New Testament as an example of faith and putting it into action. The Bible makes it clear that there is little point in having faith in God if you don't do anything about it. Being a Christian is not just about not doing wrong things, it is about doing the right things. The Bible says that God wants his people to be those who do good works, not so that they can become Christians, but because they already are.

JOE'S STORY

When he left university, Joe Fielder had the desire to do something very practical for people. He wanted to find out if his Christian faith was worth sharing and if God was relevant to people in very tough circumstances. He wanted to put his faith into action in a nitty gritty, practical way. This is his story.

'I approached an organization called Careforce which places young people in areas of great need to do voluntary Christian work. So September 1989 saw me heading to Glasgow with my knees knocking to be the youth and community worker for Ruchazie Parish Church.

'Ruchazie is a smallish housing estate which has many of the wrong social statistics: high unemployment, petty and violent crime, truancy and drug abuse. On the estate is a small church made up of local folk committed to the area and committed to showing that God cares for Ruchazie and its people.

'The people of the church decided to put their faith into action to help the unemployed and oppressed, so they started a drop in centre which I ran. We provided a cheap cafe, sports facilities and a place where the unemployed could get together to meet friends and beat the boredom. I took groups from this centre on trips and tried to start a job club to combat unemployment.

'We also started a non-alcoholic youth club called Bar-R which provided a place for the young to go and through which we tackled topics like fashion, peer pressure and violence. We wanted to show the young that their views were important and to present our views on how God could help them.

'As I worked in Ruchazie I had to struggle with thoughts like: How can a Christian talk of God's love in the face of poverty, bad housing and powerlessness? How does the truth of Jesus make a difference to a suicidal alcoholic? But over time I was able to make friends with people I would previously have run a mile from. I shared their joys, pain and frustration and was putting my faith into action.'

Ananias and Sapphira

You can't trick God

Acts 5:1-11

Aim

That the pupils would understand that the Bible teaches that God cannot be deceived.

True or False

Read out some of the true and false statements on the **Amalgam** page. Ask the pupils to vote on whether they think the statements are true or not.

Input

We might think we know a lot, but all of us fall for lies or do not believe things that are true. We have probably all at some time lied our way out of trouble, and got away with it because people believed us. In the Bible we read about a couple of people who thought they could trick God by lying to him.

Set the Scene

Put **Acts 4:32-35** into your own words to explain how the Christians were living at the time of this incident. Point out that they willingly sold property if they had some, but it was not a compulsory part of being a Christian. Go on to tell the first part of Ananias and Sapphira's story from **Acts 5:1-2**. They wanted to have the glory of being people who gave everything, without the difficulty of actually doing it, and they probably thought they would get away with deceiving the other Christians.

Banana Breaks

Prepare a banana in the following way before the assembly. Stick a pin into the banana about a third of the way down and swivel it from side to side effectively cutting the banana inside the skin. Remove the pin and repeat again about two thirds of the way down the banana.

Produce the banana and tell everyone that you are going to demonstrate the consequence of throwing a banana in the air. Throw the banana into the air three times, and then dramatically peel the banana and show that the consequence of throwing a banana is that it splits into three parts. It is worth practising this before hand to make sure you 'cut' the banana correctly.

Input

Sometimes the consequences of our actions are not what we expect them to be. Most people would not expect that the consequence of throwing a banana would be that it splits into parts. Ananias and Sapphira thought they knew what the consequence of keeping some of the money would be, but the eventual outcome was a shock to everyone.

What Really Happened

Read **Acts 5:3-11** for the rest of the story. It could be done as a dramatised reading as presented in the Dramatised Bible.

Input

What happened to Ananias and Sapphira might sound really harsh to us. But what the Bible says happened is that they deliberately tried to deceive God by pretending to give him all they had. They owned the money and they did not have to give God any of it if they did not want to, or they could have given part of the money and said that was what they were doing. But they decided to pretend to be really good, generous people yet keep some back for themselves. So the Bible says that God acted in a very definite way. He did this to show that he could not be deceived. The Bible teaches again and again that God knows everything we do and all our thoughts. God also acted in this dramatic way to demonstrate that he takes the sin of hypocrisy and lying very seriously. We might not think it matters very much, but it matters a lot to God.

Christians still believe that God cannot be deceived because he knows all that we do and think. The lesson of Ananias and Sapphira is there for us to learn: we cannot deceive God and he punishes sin very severely.

TRUE OR FALSE

The Horse Chestnut tree is so called because of the 'clip clop' noise made by conkers falling to the ground. (False)

Queen Elizabeth I passed a law obliging everyone over the age of seven to wear a flat cap on Sundays and holidays. Only lords, ladies and knights with an income of over 20 marks a year were exempt. (True)

When Sir Edmund Hillary arrived on top of Mount Everest he was surprised to see small human footprints in the snow. (False)

The Niagara Falls are turned off at night after the tourists have gone home. A hydro-electric plant upstream needs the water. (True)

During an archaeological dig in Egypt, Sir Humphrey Saville-Boyes uncovered a papyrus with a rough drawing on. The picture resembled the American space shuttle in almost every detail, but the papyrus was shown to be over 3000 years old. (False)

A greengrocer was compensated by his insurance company after his Labrador ate £80 in notes from the day's takings. (True)

In a graveyard in Suffolk are two graves dating back to the 16th century. One belongs to Oliver Hardy and the other to Stan Laurel. Local records show that they were popular comedy actors at the time of Shakespeare. (False)

Charles Osborn, of Iowa, hiccuped continuously for more than 50 years after trying to lift a 25 stone pig in 1922. (True)

In a recent traffic jam in Los Angeles, several commuters got so exasperated that they abandoned their vehicles and walked to work. When they returned to their cars in the afternoon they found the other traffic had moved on less than 1 mile. (False)

The facts marked true come from **Would You Believe This Too?** published by Coronet Books/ Hodder and Stoughton. 1975

Daniel

The cost of following God

Daniel 6

Aim

That the pupils would see that following God is costly and requires commitment.

T.V. Dinner

As the pupils enter the assembly have a video playing of lions in the wild. A clip where they are ripping apart a carcass would be good.

True Commitment

Ask for a volunteer to come to the front. They need to be a dedicated fan of a football team, a pop group or similar. Explain that you want to test their commitment and dedication, and that they can win a financial reward.

When you have your volunteer ask them if they are prepared to stand in front of the school and read the following sentence. Make it clear that they do not have to, but that if they do you will give them a reward. Start by offering a small amount such as 20p, and increase it in stages up to £2, or as much as you can afford. If they refuse to say the sentence, congratulate them on being a truly dedicated fan. If they decide it's worth it, make them read the sentence, fitting in the appropriate words, and then congratulate them on their business acumen.

'I, (say own name), think that (name of team or group) are completely useless. They have all the talent of a boiled cabbage and should retire immediately and become onion growers.'

Input

People are commited to particular teams or groups, some people more than others. In the Bible we read of someone who was committed to God with a commitment stronger than many people's.

O Worship The King?

Have the sketch from the **Amalgam** page performed. Point out how stupid the king was to sign the law so quickly without thinking of the consequences.

When people are proud, they often do things without thinking of the result, just like one of the kings in the book of Daniel.

Daniel's Commitment

The story of Daniel in the lions' den is one of the most famous stories in the Bible. If you are fairly certain that the pupils in your assembly will already know the story, you could just do a very quick summary. This will help to prevent pupils thinking they already know the story and immediately switching off. Otherwise read or tell the story as found in **chapter 6**. If you used the T.V. Dinner idea, refer back to the behaviour and viciousness of the lions. Also draw out the parallels between Darius' decision, and the law made in the sketch.

However you tell the story, focus on **chapter 6:10** which is the key verse. Point out that Daniel was sent into the den of lions because he broke the king's new law. Daniel did not have to do this. He could have stopped praying and been O.K. So why did Daniel continue praying? Explain that the Bible says that Daniel went on praying for several reasons. Daniel believed in God, and that praying was communicating with God. Daniel clearly believed that prayer was worthwhile. It got results. Daniel wanted to obey God even when that meant disobeying the king. Daniel knew that following God was costly, and he was expecting it to be difficult sometimes.

Input

Throughout the Bible it is made clear that if you decide to follow God it will be costly. The Bible never says that following God makes all your troubles go away. It can actually add some new ones, as Daniel discovered. But the Bible also says that God does not leave people to suffer alone, but is there with them in the suffering.

This is what Daniel knew which was why he prayed even in the lions' den, and we read that God answered his prayer and stopped the lions from eating him.

O WORSHIP THE KING?

His Highness Hiram Horceforth the 44th
John Paul the Courtier
Ruth Isle

(Hiram is sitting on a throne playing with his teddy. He carries on playing for a few moments. Enter John and Ruth.)

John: Your Highness Hiram Horceforth the 44th, we come to bring you news.

Hiram: Silence you impudent servant. I'm busy with Fredygo.

Ruth: Fredygo?

Hiram: Yes! Teddy Fredygo.

John: Yes, indeed, your Highness. But we bring you grave news.

Hiram: Well all right, but get on with it. It's nearly Fredygo's din-dins time.

Ruth: Well, your Highness, all the churchyards in the country are full up.

Hiram: All full up? That is grave.

Ruth: And it is going to affect us all. We're all in the same boat.

Hiram: A gravy boat I expect. Hahahahaha. Still, never mind, something will turn up. But there are more important things to worry about. Fredygo and I want our dinner, so out of my way. (The king exits taking Fredygo with him, John and Ruth bow as he leaves)

Ruth: Oh he makes me sick! Him and that stupid teddy bear.

John: It's impossible to get anything done around here. All he does is play with that stupid bear. I tell you, I'd like to get my hands on that bear and ring its neck.

Ruth: Well that may be possible. I've just had a cunning plan, listen. (They walk off whispering conspiratorially. Enter Hiram and Fredygo, Hiram sits on the throne. Ruth and John enter carrying a piece of paper and a pen)

Ruth: Your Highness Hiram Horceforth the 44th!

Hiram: What is it, Miss Isle?

Ruth: Your Highness, we believe that you alone are the most important person in the whole kingdom.

John: But some people don't know it, and consequently do not adore you as their king.

Ruth: So we think that you ought to pass a law to say that anybody who worships anything other than you, will have their object of worship destroyed.

Hiram: Good idea, good idea. How dare these ungrateful subjects worship anything other than me.

Ruth: We have already drafted the law so if you would like to sign... (She presents Hiram with the paper and pen and he signs immediately)

Hiram: (To Fredygo) Aren't I a clever king? Making all these good laws. If everybody had a teddy like you, why there would be no problem. You're the best person in all the world Fredygo.

Ruth: Um, your highness?

Hiram: What is it now? I'm looking after Fredygo.

John: We are sad to tell your highness that we have found somebody breaking the law already.

Hiram: Strewth! Ruth, tell me the truth.

Ruth: It is true, somebody is worshipping something other than you.

Hiram: Well destroy this object, whatever it is. Use whatever measures you need, let nothing stand in your way.

John: Then, your highness, we demand that you hand over Fredygo immediately. You are guilty of worshipping something other than yourself, so we must destroy him. (They seize the teddy and Ruth produces a pair of scissors. She flourishes them grandly and then cuts up the teddy)

Hiram: Noooooooo!! (He sits sobbing on the throne. John and Ruth leave laughing)

Jonathan

Friendship and loyalty

1 Samuel 20

Aim

That the pupils would see that the Bible gives us a blueprint for good friendships.

Instructions

Ask for three volunteers who want to win a prize. Give each person a pen and a piece of paper, and ask them to draw what you describe to them. Then describe the picture from the **Amalgam** page. Do this quickly to avoid boredom. If you go too fast for the pupils, do not worry as it will add to the humour. Award a prize for the most accurate drawing.

Input

The drawings could have been better if the artists were given clearer instructions. We spend a lot of our life reading instructions, such as how to work the video, or how to play a game. If we want to get things right, we need to read the instructions. Christians believe that the Bible is God's instruction book for life. One part of life for which it gives us instructions is friendship.

You Love Yourself

Have a bag containing a selection of toiletries. Get as many as possible covering many different parts of the body. For example, shampoo, nail scissors, foot powder, a razor and so on. Explain that you were looking in a chemist's and were amazed at how many things there were to help people look good. Produce the items one at a time getting faster as you go on.

Input

Manufacturers make so many products because they know that we love looking after ourselves. When the Bible talks about friendship, it also talks about loving yourself, not in a vain way that is to do with how you look, but having self respect and value in God's sight.

David and Jonathan

Tell the story of David and Jonathan. Either read it from **1 Samuel 20**, or use the outline below:

Saul was king of Israel and became jealous of David. David seemed to have all the gifts and talents that Saul lacked, so Saul decided to kill him. David became aware of this and so he got his best friend, Jonathan, to find out what was going on. Jonathan was in a good position to know because he was Saul's son.

They drew up a plan for Jonathan to carry out at the New Moon Festival. He would see how Saul reacted to David being absent, and then they would know what the king was planning. David would stay in hiding and Jonathan would give him the answer.

Before the festival they promised to be faithful to each other. Jonathan was prepared to risk his father's anger because he was great friends with David. He was as concerned for David's safety as he was for his own. The next day they put the plan into action. King Saul was furious that David was not at the festivities and threw his spear at Jonathan to try and kill him. So Jonathan passed the message on to David so that he could escape.

Input

Jonathan was a great friend. He risked everything for David including his life. Eventually he helped David escape. He wanted him to be safe even if it meant not seeing him again.

Jonathan was a selfless person. The Bible says that Jonathan loved David as much as he loved himself, but to have that respect for David he had to have self respect as well. If he did not think much of himself, he could not think much of David.

The Bible teaches that God designed friendship to be selfless and loving. God wants us to have self respect and to treat others as we treat ourselves, just as Jonathan did. The Bible also says that the best friend we could ever have is someone who always wants the best for us, and gives up everything for us, including their life. The Bible says that only one person has done that – Jesus.

How do I start and finish an assembly?

Getting the pupils' attention is notoriously difficult, but losing their attention and then trying to regain it is doubly hard. So how do you go about making sure they are with you right from the start? Then, when you have finished what happens? Do you all just wander out of the hall, or is there more for the pupils to think about and do?

The first 30 seconds of what you say or do are vital. You can either get the pupils' interest or lose it then. A snappy, confident beginning will keep their interest and give you a good start for the rest of the assembly. The introduction needs to be carefully planned so you do not have to stop and think what to say. If you are new to the school, introduce yourself, as no one likes being talked to by an anonymous person. Keep your introduction short – a detailed description of your job and home will not interest many of the pupils.

If you are a regular visitor, try to make the start of each assembly different. The unexpected is a good way to gain people's attention. You could start with a question. For example, you could start the assembly on Job on page 31 with, 'Why does God allow suffering?' If you are starting with an activity, launch straight into the activity and then introduce the subject. This will mean that the pupils will be wanting to know why the activity was done and will be waiting for you to carry on. Similarly, if you are using a sketch, you could have the sketch performed before you start the assembly.

Another method is to appear preoccupied with something else and ignore the pupils for a few seconds. For this to work you need to be totally engrossed in an activity, such as setting up the Faveometer in the Cornelius assembly on page 21. As you continue to be busy the pupils will want to know what is taking all your attention, so will be waiting for your explanation. Using different areas of the hall will help to get the pupils' attention. Start from the back of the hall and walk to the front as you talk, or sit in the middle of the pupils and then climb out and work your way to the front. All these suggestions will help get attention. They need to be planned beforehand, and then backed up by carefully prepared input.

Almost any assembly can be quite good, but the mark of a really effective assembly is what happens afterwards. Do the pupils forget everything? Or will the assembly be discussed at lunch time? How the assembly ends will greatly affect its impact. Timing is crucial; if you have overrun you will lose the pupils' attention. If there is a system of bells, the pupils will start to pack their bags and get ready to go as soon as the bell rings.

Plan your concluding remark. You might want to finish with a question or a challenge rising out of the assembly. At the end of the assembly on Peter on page 41 you could ask, 'Are you prepared to forgive people, the way Jesus forgave Peter?' If you are going to ask a question or give a challenge, make sure the pupils do not go away feeling guilty if they cannot live up to it. If you are doing a series of assemblies, prepare the way for the next one, even to the extent of saying, 'But to find that out, you will have to wait until next time!' If you are closing with a prayer, have a few seconds' pause after the prayer and before you hand over to a staff member. Always thank the pupils for allowing you to take their assembly.

REMEMBER

- **The first 30 seconds are vital.**
- **If you are new to the school introduce yourself.**
- **The unexpected is a good way to gain people's attention.**
- **The mark of a really effective assembly is what happens afterwards.**
- **Always thank the pupils for allowing you to take their assembly.**

How can I link assemblies into my youth work?

So you turn up every now and then to take an assembly. Great! The work is beginning to prove worthwhile in its own right. Fantastic! But what is the connection between what you do for fifteen minutes at the start of a school day and your on-going church youth work? If the answer is 'none', read on.

It would be helpful, first of all, to be sure there are no connections. Will some of your church youth group be there in school, as pupils? Do members of your church teach at the school? Are members of your church on the Board of Governors? Try and find any connections that can work to your advantage.

Raise the profile of Christians in schools by getting them to take part in assemblies, by interviewing them, or by getting them to tell their own stories. I have known this to enable one young Christian teacher to realise she was not the only Christian in the school. It will certainly take the particular individual into some evangelistic opportunities during the day. They need to be armed with invitation cards to the church/youth group/guest service or whatever.

But let's assume the worst. You've searched for a link and can't find any. You need to have a realistic expectation that you cannot evangelize and disciple the whole school through assemblies. If there is a Christian Union at the school things can go a little further, but eventually those who are interested in the Gospel need to be encouraged to make a link with their local church.

This begs the next question; where do we do assemblies? In most State schools the pupils will all come from a clearly defined geographical area and a link can be made with one or two local churches, which you probably already know well. When schools cover wider areas, you will need to develop a working knowledge of churches that are sympathetic to young people and will welcome them.

You may be invited to take assemblies as a 'hit and run' raid. That is to say, invited on a special occasion as a one-off. Make connections with local churches by having something else to invite people to, and some literature to give out. Schools are often sympathetic to publicizing church events, so arrange for posters advertising youth events to be put up in as many local schools as possible. Make a point of drawing attention to them in assemblies, or asking someone else to.

It is good to use young people from the youth group to help with assemblies. If they go to different schools permission can usually be obtained for them to be absent for a short time to help in assemblies. If members of your youth group have musical gifts this can be used to advantage. Make sure they are used in their own schools as well.

Above all other things, it is important to present your church youth work as important. Give it a positive image. Refer to it a lot. Enthuse about the things you are doing. If you are undertaking projects then share them with schools and ask for help. One youth group I worked with tackled the 'Christmas Cracker' project and local schools were a great source of the things needed to set up a Third World Restaurant. A number of young people got involved in the youth group because they were interested in the project. A small number became Christians.

Linking your assemblies with the rest of your youth work is not possible overnight. You need to make the links again and again in order to see fruit. Changing the image of the church in the eyes of young people is a five year aim rather than an immediately achievable goal. Keep plugging away.

REMEMBER

- **Find out if you already have connections with some pupils.**
- **Raise the profile of Christians in the school by involving them where possible.**
- **Publicize church events when possible.**
- **Use young people from the youth group to help with assemblies.**
- **Give your church youth work a positive image.**

How can I pray in assemblies?

Assemblies are supposed to be a collective act of worship, and as part of this, many people include prayer in their assemblies. But how many of the pupils join in or understand what prayer is? However, prayer can be a valuable and significant part of an assembly. Below are some ideas to help you explore the use of prayer in your assemblies.

Any prayer time needs to be genuine, and we need to set the example of how to pray. The pupils will tell the difference between praying and reading or reciting a prayer. If we genuinely pray in assemblies on a regular basis, it will help the pupils understand that we believe we are talking to God, not just saying empty words.

We also need to respect those who don't want to pray for any reason, be it that they are from another religion or that they don't believe in God. It is a matter of courtesy and respect to allow these pupils to sit quietly while we pray. It will also show pupils and staff that we are sensitive towards the pupils' personal beliefs, and this can be a powerful witness in itself. One way to help pupils choose whether to pray is to spell it out clearly before you begin. You could say something like, 'I'm going to pray now. If you want to pray, then join in saying 'Amen' at the end. If you don't want to, then just sit quietly'. It can feel clumsy saying this kind of thing regularly, but if we do it reinforces the idea that praying is an active thing so people need to be free to opt out if they prefer.

We need to watch our language when we are praying. It is very easy to use Christian jargon which the pupils may not understand. We need to remember that part of what we are doing is leading them in prayer. Plan the prayers beforehand, not to take away any natural feeling but to steer clear of jargon.

In our survey, most of the young people found assemblies boring and often irrelevant. We need to make sure that prayer does not fall into those categories, and that there are ways to communicate the prayers to help the pupils respond to what is happening. Slides or a video could be shown just before or during your prayers. You could show something to demonstrate the majesty of God, such as a wildlife programme, or there may be a particular video linked to the topic of the assembly. Having something visual whilst you are praying also means the pupils can keep their eyes open. Many pupils find it embarrassing to close their eyes in public. Some music could be played to help create the right atmosphere for the prayer time. This could be almost anything from lively, punchy music to meditative chants such as the music produced by the Taize community.

There may be opportunities to use set prayers or even parts of our church liturgy. One advantage of using these on occasions is that if the pupils come to church, there will be parts of the service they will know. That will help them to feel more confident in a church service.

There may be pupils that we can involve in leading prayers. The principle here is the same as if you are leading the prayers. The pupils need to be helped to see that they are praying and not just reading prayers. To help pupils understand this will make a difference to the prayers they pray, and to themselves as they pray them.

A final idea that might seem daft is silence. Few young people have space in their lives for quiet. A short time spent in quiet can be a valuable and significant part of the day. An occasional short time of silence will almost certainly be appreciated by the pupils more than we realise.

REMEMBER

- **Pray sincerely.**
- **Allow pupils the chance not to pray.**
- **Avoid Christian jargon.**
- **Keep the prayers interesting.**
- **Use different forms of communication in the prayers.**

How can I use testimonies in assemblies?

Having someone in an assembly describing what God has done in their lives can be a powerful and fascinating exercise which really brings Christianity to life. However, it can be deadly dull and a turn-off if it is not handled correctly. Many of the pupils questioned in the survey liked having different visitors, and people who told them about themselves. This interest in real people's lives can be used effectively in the assembly situation.

If you want to have someone giving their testimony think carefully about who you invite. They need, not only to have something to say, but also to be able to communicate with the pupils. You may want to go for someone the pupils will know and be able to relate to, such as a member of staff, or someone who would be an interesting visitor, perhaps a doctor or an astronaut! Don't be tempted just to go for young lively people – some more elderly people have fascinating accounts to give and are quite capable of communicating naturally with the pupils. The pupils will be far more interested in an honest and genuine account than a false comedy show.

Who you select will also depend on what you want them to talk about. You may want them to give an account of how they became a Christian, but there are lots of other aspects of the Christian life which you can also highlight through testimony. You might want them to give an account of how God helped them through a particularly difficult time in their lives, or how he has been faithful to them over the years. You could draw out the difference being a Christian has made to them in their lives.

How the person delivers their testimony is also something you can vary. They may be confident enough to give a straight talk. If they are going to do this, make sure they understand the assembly situation. They will need to know how long they can speak for, the numbers and kinds of pupils who will be there and the type of language and illustrations they can use. If they are new to doing assemblies invite them to come along to one with you first to observe what happens.

Another method is to interview the person. This means that you have some control over the situation to avoid them overrunning and to bring out the points you want to raise. If you are going to interview them go through what you are going to ask first so that they can think about their answers. Very few people are capable of thinking up answers on the spot that are worth listening to. Whilst you are doing the interview try to position yourselves in such a way that the two of you have some eye contact. This will help you to cut in on a answer if you need to. It also makes it more like an interview where the idea is basically that the two of you are having a conversation and everyone else is eavesdropping. If you are doing an interview it is also possible to interview more than one person. So you could interview someone brought up as a Christian and someone who was converted later in life and show the differences in their lives but the similarity of the work of God.

However you choose to use testimonies in an assembly, make sure that what your guest says fits in with the rest of the assembly. This means that you will need to plan your assembly before you invite someone. Doing this will ensure that everything that happens in the assembly dovetails together.

REMEMBER

- **Think carefully about who you invite.**
- **Plan your assembly before you invite someone.**
- **Make sure that what your guest says fits in with the rest of the assembly.**
- **Make sure that your guest understands the assembly situation.**

How can I plan a series of assemblies?

Following the article on **Nuts and Bolts** page 6, here are some extra ideas on how to plan a series of assemblies. Many of the ideas here use some of the assemblies in **Assembly Line**, and then go on to develop the idea.

Because you cannot guarantee having all the same young people in every assembly in a series, it is important to make sure that each assembly makes a self-contained point, as well as being linked to the others in the series. Some ways of linking the main points for a series are:

Continuing Bible Material

These can be based around as much, or as little, Bible material as you want. 'The whole Bible in two assemblies' is a real possibility, as is 'Seven sessions on Creation'. To do either of those requires the same clear thinking about exactly what the main point of each assembly is, and how the Bible material will be put across. A good way to start would be to choose one of the assemblies in **Assembly Line**, use that as one of the series, and plan a couple of others to go with it on the same Bible character – Peter, Moses or Martha would be good ones to try.

Continuing Story

Another possibility is to use a non-Biblical story which is continued between sessions. This can be done using drama or by another means of storytelling. It is necessary to do 'the story so far' at the beginning – not as a boring recap of everything that has gone before, but as a quick, punchy, attention-getter.

Ideas are: the life of a real Christian (these need to be honest – not just full of wonderful happenings!), adapting a Christian book (e.g. Screwtape Letters), or creating a drama which retells the Gospel story using fictional characters in a setting more familiar to the young people. See **Nuts & Bolts** page 60 for more ideas.

Begging the Question

This type of series begins with a question which the first assembly tries to answer. But answering it begs another question, which is then taken on next time. This is a good way of dealing with some of the big questions which young people have.

For example:

1 'Why does God allow suffering?'
2 'Is God in control?'
3 'Why does God let us have a choice?'
4 'Why doesn't God get rid of the people who make the wrong choice?'

Theme

Another way of using the outlines in **Assembly Line** to create a series of assemblies is to build on their themes. For example:

Big Mistakes: 1 Achan, **2** Belshazzar, **3** Peter

Jesus is for Everyone: 1 Prejudice, **2** Jonah, **3** Cornelius, **4** Christians all over the world

You could create a theme which picks up on any particular comments which pupils in the school have made, or things which fit the circumstances of the school or assemblies particularly well. For example:

Fears: 1 I'm afraid of the future. **2** I'm afraid of being alone. **3** I'm afraid of myself. **4** I'm afraid of dying.

One Point

An alternative to linking the main points of a series of assemblies into a theme is to have just one main point for the whole series. It is important then to put it across in very different ways each time so that you are not being boring. This approach helps to avoid problems of continuity. Effectively it is like having one big assembly spread over several sessions.

Having a series of assemblies might seem like hard work and extra planning, but they can bring great benefits to the overall style and content of your assemblies. Have a look at the other **Nuts & Bolts** pages for more creative ideas on how to communicate in the assemblies.

REMEMBER

- **Make sure that each assembly makes a self-contained point.**
- **Make sure that each assembly is linked to the others in the series.**
- **Use the assemblies in Assembly Line as a basis for a series.**

How can I involve the pupils in assemblies?

When asked, many pupils will say that they like to be involved in assemblies and to feel a part of them. But when the crunch comes and they have to stand up in front of the other pupils it can be a different story. However, getting the pupils involved can help to really bring the assembly alive and keep the pupils interested in what is going on.

There are different ways that you can involve pupils. You might have some peforming a sketch or praying, or you might want to be brave and ask for 'live' volunteers to be involved in an activity. This is more risky: What happens if nobody volunteers? How will they act in front of the other pupils? Will they bring out the point you want to make? You might think that with these risks it is not worth bothering, but doing something that involves some risk will bring an assembly to life. It will also make the assembly memorable and enjoyable.

If you want volunteers, you need to ask for them in a way that sounds appealing and not embarrassing. Offering prizes such as sweets or cans of drink is a good way of encouraging participants. Think about what you want the volunteers to do and work out a wording to announce it. 'Two volunteers to demonstrate their bravery and courage and win a prize', could be the way you announce the 'Totally Trustworthy Test' from the Abraham assembly on page 17.

When using volunteers make sure they do not feel embarrassed or belittled. Explain clearly what you want them to do, and make sure they understand before you start. Always praise the volunteers for what they have done, even if they have failed the activity. Do not always ask for applause, as the other pupils might not be keen to give it and this can be embarrassing. Making the volunteers feel good about joining in, and showing appreciation for what they have done, will make pupils more confident to volunteer next time.

When you use volunteers you need to make sure that the rest of the pupils also feel involved. Make sure that everyone can see what is happening and do a running commentary. If you are asking questions make sure everyone can hear the answers. Either use a microphone or repeat all the answers. You could play music in the background as the activity is happening, or even have a video camera linked into a television and do a video link. Position the television so that the other pupils can see, and then you can have close ups of the volunteers in action. If you have access to a video camera this can be quite easy to set up and very effective to use. You will need to have someone with you to operate the camera.

You might want to get all the pupils involved in an activity such as 'Total Control' from the Jonah assembly on page 27. These are fun but again involve some of the risks involved in using volunteers. There are other ways you can involve all the pupils, for example having half of a sketch performed and then asking the pupils what they think is going to happen. Find out what they would do in the situation, then go back to see the conclusion. This can also be done using video clips.

These ideas do require confidence, but they are things that pupils want to have happening in assemblies. If you want to give them a go but lack the confidence to launch straight in, start with activities which use all the pupils. Rehearse beforehand what you are going to do, and run the activity through with people you know to see if they understand and can cope with the activity. Have a contingency plan just in case nobody does volunteer. This is unlikely but it can be reassuring to have one. Perhaps do the activity yourself, or tell the pupils what would have happened and then move on to the next part of the assembly. Above all, do not worry if nobody volunteers. It might be embarassing, but you can still deliver a good, relevant assembly.

REMEMBER

- **Use volunteers – it involves risks, but is worthwhile.**
- **Offer prizes.**
- **Do not embarrass the volunteers.**
- **Make sure the other pupils feel involved.**
- **Do not worry if it does not go according to plan.**

How can I create the right atmosphere in assemblies?

You arrive in a cold hall and face 100 bored pupils, so you launch into your assembly. Within a few minutes the place is full of merriment. By the end of the assembly your every comment gets a laugh and after your closing prayer you get a spontaneous cheer. The atmosphere has been exciting, but as the teachers drag the hyped-up pupils off to their lessons you get the feeling that they are not impressed with your assembly technique.

So what has gone wrong? The assembly was not boring and certainly will not be forgotten, but it has fallen into the trap of winding up the pupils at the start of the day. When you lead an assembly, particularly if you are a visitor in a school, you need to remember that the pupils have a day's lessons ahead of them, and the chances are they will be going straight to a lesson where they will be required to study hard. Teachers will have a real job on their hands if the pupils arrive so excited that they need a couple of hours to calm down. When creating an atmosphere in an assembly you need to have the teachers in mind as well. Is your assembly improving the teachers' day as well as the pupils'? If it is, then your assembly will be far more effective. This does not mean that the assembly cannot be fun, but it needs to be controlled.

Although the atmosphere does not want to get out of control it does want to have life in it. This does not mean being lively every time, but thinking carefully and creatively about the kind of atmosphere you want. You may want to have an assembly where there is an atmosphere of wonder and amazement at God's creation, or you may be called to take an assembly at a particular time of sadness or thanksgiving, and in those situations it is important to create the right atmosphere.

When planning your assembly, bear in mind the atmosphere you want to create, and plan things that can help you build it. Is there any particular music that can be playing as the pupils enter? Many schools have the facility to have music playing and you may be able to use this. Are there pictures or other visual aids you could display for the pupils to look at? Simple things like candles can be very powerful for the pupils just to look at (and attempt to blow out – they need to be kept at a distance).

If you are doing a series of assemblies try to have variety in the atmospheres. If every time you go they are very lively and upbeat, they will soon lose their cutting edge. But if one has a calmer atmosphere it will stand out as being different.

You will also need to be adaptable as the atmosphere will be controlled to a certain extent by circumstances outside your control. There may have been notices about litter, or a prize giving, before you start so you will then need to work at creating a different atmosphere if you want one. These are things you will become familiar with if you are a regular visitor to the school. If you are just doing one assembly in a school it would be worth visiting beforehand to get a feel for the usual atmosphere in the assemblies.

Creating atmospheres is not about manipulating pupils in assemblies. It becomes manipulation when the atmosphere is forced and gets the pupils hyped-up. It is important to avoid this and this can be done by being natural and genuine, and not building up such an atmosphere that it becomes an emotional high. All assemblies will have an atmosphere; the important thing is to recognize this and to build a positive one.

REMEMBER

- **Make the atmosphere in your assembly a positive one.**
- **Do not hype the pupils up so that the teachers have to calm them down again.**
- **Create the atmosphere throughout the whole assembly.**
- **Have variety in the atmospheres you create.**
- **Be natural at all times.**

How can I use soap operas in assemblies?

Among the most watched programmes on television are soap operas. The on-going stories and regular characters make them favourite forms of entertainment. It is possible to use and adapt this interest in assemblies.

If you are taking assemblies on a regular basis you can build your own soap opera into your presentation. Your regular visits will give you the opportunity to establish characters and leave 'cliff hangers' for you to resolve at the start of your next assembly. Finding pictures for each character will enable you to use these each time, so that the pupils become familiar with the story line.

Writing a soap opera can take time, but if it is written all at one time it will save on the actual week-by-week preparation for the assemblies. When writing a story you could either write episodes that illustrate a particular point such as the danger of pride or the consequence of sin, or you could write one which is an allegory of an actual story. An obvious choice for this is the Gospel story as found in one of the four gospels. By writing an allegory much of the work is done for you. You select the bits you want to tell and then change the characters' names and their situation to fit your soap opera. The following example uses a Robin Hood theme and is based on St. Matthew's gospel.

Characters:	*Biblical equivalent*
The hooded man –	*Jesus*
Will Scarlet (narrator) –	*Matthew*
John Little –	*John the Baptist*
Friar Tuck –	*Matthew*
Friar Sausage –	*Andrew*
Sue and Don Pling –	*James and John*
Maid Marion –	*Judas*
The sheriff –	*Satan*
Sir Guy –	*Pilate*
Soldiers –	*Romans*
Priests –	*Jews*

Episode 1. People get ready.

From Matthew 1:18-25 , Matthew 2:13-18 and Matthew 3:1-12 .

Will Scarlet introduces the story. Will is a tax collector who has offices above the Pole and Staff Tavern in Nottingham (people had to pay Pole Tax!). He tells the story in the first person, and was told to write it down as he was the only one who could write.

'For years the country has been under the rule of a tyrant: the Sheriff of Nottingham. Many people, including Jerry Myah and Easy Kiel, have come and promised that the Sheriff will be overthrown. Things started to really happen about 33 years ago. I wasn't born then, but my mum's told me all about it. Apparently some kings came from the East, Ipswich or somewhere, and said they'd come to see the new king. But instead of going up to the sheriff's castle, they went to a house on David Street. When the sheriff heard, he lost his temper, and had all the children killed. Apparently the family the kings had visited heard of his plan and fled abroad. They stayed in Wales for a while before returning.

Not much happened for a few years and then a man called John Little started preaching in the streets. He said similar things to those Jerry Myah and Easy Kiel had said. The promise was going to come true and someone was going to save everyone from the sheriff. He also said that everyone had to get ready for him by being washed in the river Trent. Unbelievably lots of people went with him. However, when some of the priests went out to see what was going on, he accused them of being hypocrites and said they would be the first to get the chop. Everyone thought John Little was going to get arrested when out of the trees walked a hooded figure. Everyone turned to look at him. 'Who is this man?' they all asked...'.

This was a ten episode soap opera and was used on a venture for young people. It was immensely popular and helped the young people to see the Gospel in a new way. Explaining the story was left to individual chats, and in a school situation could be dealt with after the last episode or in RE lessons. The advantage of doing this is that it allows the story to speak for itself, and lets the young people try and work out what is going to happen.

Was that assembly any good?

An important, and often overlooked, aspect of taking assemblies is evaluation. Evaluation means more than just thinking 'that seemed to go OK', and it is one of the ways that you can begin to improve your assembly skills.

Before you start evaluating you need to know what the aim of the assembly is. You can then find out if you achieved the aim. You need to make your aims realistic, but at the same time give yourself something to go for. So to aim for no one to fall asleep is probably not going to stretch you very far, but to aim for everyone to fully understand the gospel of John is rather unrealistic. You also need to make your aims 'learner centred'. This means that when you decide on your aim you will have the pupils, not yourself, in mind. It will mean the difference between an aim which says:

That you will teach about sin;

and one which says:

That the pupils will understand the seriousness and consequences of sin.

This may sound like playing with words, but it affects evaluation. Take that first aim – you may well have taught about sin. But did the pupils grasp what you were saying? In considering the second aim you need to ask, 'Did I explain sin in such a way that they will have been able to understand?' This form of evaluation is harder, but it is ultimately more useful for us and the pupils who will hear us next time.

It is often quite hard to evaluate effectively if you are involved in writing and presenting an assembly. Learning to evaluate and knowing which questions to ask yourself take time, but there are ways you can begin.

Is there a person you can ask to evaluate your assembly? There may be a member of staff who could sit in and take notes for you. If there is nobody in the school, is there someone who could go in with you? If you take someone with you always explain to a staff member who they are and why they are with you, as a matter of courtesy and to reassure the staff that it is you being evaluated and not them.

In all this the people who really matter are the pupils, and there are ways that you can get feedback from them. We will look at response during the assembly in a moment, but you can also find out from them afterwards. This needs to be approached in the right way. Just rushing up to a group of pupils and saying 'What did you think of my assembly then?' will probably illicit some embarrassed shuffling and a few 'OK' type comments. It may be that teachers can help you by finding out later on what the pupils learnt and enjoyed from the assembly. If you are going to be taking some lessons, do the same thing. But do not ask questions about how you personally did, or many will be too embarrassed to answer.

During the assembly you can evaluate its success. Obvious things like: Did anyone laugh? How many fell asleep? But don't put too much score on this. Young adolescents are notorious for not responding in assemblies. Many are self conscious and will be embarrassed to laugh out loud. But there are more subtle things to look for. Are people looking at you, or the clock? Are they attentive or restless? Is the atmosphere one of attentiveness or just quiet?

All these are things you need to be aware of as you lead an assembly, and again they are things which an observer might be able to notice for you. But there is no point in just evaluating an assembly. If it is going to be worthwhile you need to respond to your conclusions.

REMEMBER

- **Set your aim first.**
- **Keep it 'learner centred'.**
- **Be objective afterwards.**
- **Use other people if it's helpful.**
- **Always try and get feedback from the pupils.**

Start your aims like this:

- **'That the pupils would learn that...',**
- **'That the pupils would understand...',**
- **'That the pupils would realize that...'**

A checklist of things to do

Now that you have read this resource you are ready to launch into your next assembly! Here is a checklist of things to remember. These have been culled from various sources and founts of wisdom.

1. **If you have not done an assembly in the school before, speak to a member of staff who normally takes assemblies and check how the routine operates and the way you would fit into it. Better still, go and watch an assembly take place.**
2. **Ensure that there will be someone to hand over to when you have concluded your part of the assembly.**
3. **Make sure any equipment you are going to use works, and set it up before you start.**
4. **Make sure your activities and input meet your aim for the assembly.**
5. **If you involve anyone from the audience be confident and do not embarrass them.**
6. **Make sure everyone can see and hear you.**
7. **Be punctual and keep strictly to the allocated time slot.**
8. **Keep the message straightforward.**
9. **Relax and speak in a normal fashion.**
10. **Always support the staff of the school.**

Useful people and resources

Addresses

Association of Christian Teachers
Stapleford House Education Centre
ACT
Wesley Place
Stapleford
Nottingham NG9 8DP

Pathfinders
CPAS
Athena Drive
Tachbrook Park
WARWICK CV34 6NG
Sales (01926) 334242

CTVC
Hillside Studios,
Merry Hill Road
Bushey
Watford
HERTFORDSHIRE WD2 1DR

Scripture Union in Schools
130 City Road
London EC1V 2NJ

Resources

Blood and Honey video, produced by CTVC.

Stop and Think. Collective worship for Secondary schools video. produced by CTVC.

Compass. Bible-based teaching resource for use with 11s-14s, published by CPAS / Pathfinders.

Growing More like Jesus. Bible-based teaching resource for use with 12s-16s, published by CPAS / Pathfinders. Product code 16121.

All Together Forever. Bible-based teaching resource for use with 12s-16s, published by CPAS / Pathfinders. Product code 16122.

CPAS resources are available by mail order from the above address.

Dramatised Bible published by Marshall Pickering: Bible Society.

Leading Worship in Schools by Janet King. Published by Monarch Publications.

52 Ideas for Secondary School Assemblies edited by Janet King. Published by Monarch Publications.

Assembly Point by Grahame Knox and David Lawrence. Published by British Youth for Christ and Scripture Union.

A Really Great Assembly by Grahame Knox and Chris Chesterton. Published by British Youth for Christ and Scripture Union.